Lifelines

Sane Meditations for a Mad World

Geraint. D. Fielder

CHRISTIAN FOCUS

Copyright © Geraint D. Fielder 2005

ISBN 1-84550-029-6

10 9 8 7 6 5 4 3 2 1

First published in 2005
by
Christian Focus Publications,
Geanies House, Fearn,
Ross-shire, IV20 1TW, Scotland

www.christianfocus.com

Cover design by Alister MacInnes

Printed and bound by
CPD, Wales

Contents

Invitation to Life

Life's End or New Beginnings?

(Each chapter began as a radio or television broadcast)

Preface

He lived in South Wales. He was usually up before 6.30am This particular morning he got up intending to leave his wife for another woman. He put the radio on while shaving. It was 6.25 am. *Prayer for the Day* was going out and he heard the story of Joseph resisting the temptation of an affair. It so arrested him that he contacted the broadcaster. The eventual result was the reconciliation of husband and wife.

Response to 'A Social Worker's Nightmare' (p. 7)

An Oxfordshire couple had given up on their marriage and were living in separate parts of the house, waiting for their divorce to go through. The man found himself listening to the Sunday Morning Service. It spoke of how Christ could bring down walls between people in the home. He began to cry and went to tell his wife about the broadcast. She was listening to the same programme and weeping herself. They cancelled their solicitors and made a new start.

Response to 'Love Never Fails' (p. 40)

"My husband died after four years of fighting against a kidney disease...I have really tried to thank God for my blessings around me. Yet through it all I have been so lost and alone...for years I have only touched lightly on the truth. I think I have been like Thomas, so doubting all the time. Life too had lost its meaning for me. Now I wish to tell you that yesterday's service gave me the strength I've needed. What I will do now is to reread my New Testament and then I shall get nearer and nearer to a real living Jesus."

Response to 'Incline Your Ear' (p. 181)

"I was driving around in my car looking for cut price petrol, and turning on the radio, found your programme which was worth the whole year's license fee. We are a firm...whose task is to persuade management and employees to work in harmony to solve specific problems. So your sermon on harmony was of special significance. I would very much like to quote it during my forthcoming lectures."

Response to 'Harmony' (p. 173)

Responses like these persuaded me to turn my broadcasts into a book. Having heard them, many had asked for them in more permanent form. The talks were given over many years and in many kinds of Christian broadcasting slots on BBC radio and television. I have organized them under five fundamental themes of the Christian faith and life. They are, however, all still self-contained and you can dip in at any point, or settle down for a longer read. For those of you who heard them on air, they may reinforce the message.

The broadcasts and television transmissions from church congregations were joyous and exciting events—you may have been there—one among many Christians who sought to pass on to millions their faith in the Risen Christ as Saviour and Lord. Sunday programmes like Radio 4's Sunday Morning Service, or Radio Wales' Celebration can be an uplifting experience and I recall with gratitude to God the congregations of Whitefield Presbyterian Church, Abergavenny; Highfields Free Church, Cardiff; Glenwood Community Church, Cardiff; Moriah Baptist Chapel, Risca; The University of Wales Medical School Christian Fellowship; and the choir and choir master of St Asaph's Cathedral, North Wales. The broadcasts are over, but the book has come. The swiftly moving flow of all those past events have now been captured and put within our hands, available for study and meditation and providing, I hope, an enjoyable read.

Rendering the spoken word into written material is a subtle work and requires editorial skills. I thank Philip Ross for his help in turning broadcasts into a book.

I dedicate this book to the delights of my life—Mary, Martyn, Robert, David and Cherry—all of whom have encouraged me, and each other, in Christ.

Acknowledgements

I acknowledge debt to the writings of many, including Jay Adams, Ian Barclay, Herman Bavinck, O. Hallesby, David Ingram, Derek Kidner, C. S. Lewis, Douglas Macmillan, Peter Masters, Derek Llwyd Morgan, J. I. Packer, James Philip, Francis Schaeffer, Michael Schlutter, Helmut Thielicke, David Watson, John White. Their ideas and words lie scattered throughout and I am grateful.

Our Flawed Life

1

Conversion and the Real World

The word 'conversion' constantly comes up in daily conversation—converting our holiday currency; converting a house into student flats; someone converting a try in rugby; converting, or not, to the Euro.

Conversion is also a great Christian word. But surely it's useless in the real world that hits us each Monday morning.

Can Christian conversion affect the real world out there? Hard. Cynical. Disillusioned. Cut-throat, rat-race, treadmill-driven; at once violent and indulgent, unforgiving and sometimes, oh so lonely. It makes you long for more signs of human warmth, real appreciation. In other words, the real world needs a change of heart, doesn't it? A change for the better—a conversion no less.

To put it bluntly, the real world could do with a dose of healthy four letter words—words like care, hope, help, love. A world of kind, good, true people, where children are safe—safe to walk home alone from school—and where adults are pure in motive and action.

Is it vain to work for such a change of heart, a change for the better in such a world? I believe conversion to Jesus Christ, the Saviour of the world, is the precondition that makes such a change possible. I am persuaded of that. A world on the mend requires converted people, a people who turn to God. Without that, standards will continue to slide.

Whoever we are, city financier or the girl at the checkout, the sleepless mum or the absentee dad, the stressed out teacher or her overcrowded class, the unwell or the fighting fit, the sexploiter on the Internet or the cult leader, the kinky cleric or just ordinary flawed you and me, all of us, any of us—we can all do with a radical rescue and a deep down renewing. Many find that renewing, in practice, in a turn round to Christ as Lord and an openness to all that is true and good in him.

Without that source of those virtues and values, care, love and help runs dry in our real world, but given the right conditions, they are still available to us. They flourish in what Jesus shows to be the real world—the kingdom of God. And to belong there, he reminds us, requires conversion.

2

The Weekend

Lots of us look forward to a nice weekend: fun with the family, a potter in the garden or a game of rugby — a chance to press the pause button. A time to recover, relax, or even reflect on life's priorities.

It's easy to lose this knack of reflection, especially if we've lost the habit of listening to the age-old weekend word — the word of the Lord.

Without that, we lose our hold on the spiritual resources and values we need. It causes all kinds of weekend family crises and it's rough on the children. Weekend breaks are great. But doesn't that nice weekend or happy home so often elude us? We put in extra working hours, build high hopes for the weekend and get a flat disappointment. Perhaps the children go sick, the car breaks down. Somehow you haven't the spiritual resources to cope and, one day, snap — the weekend break leads instead to breakdown. Simple crises become the fuse that explodes bigger worries of mortgage rates, soaring bills, or sudden redundancy.

A prophet sees the causes of a crisis and gives a word from God about it. The prophet Haggai lived in days of galloping inflation. In a famous phrase he said, 'You earn wages only to put them in a purse with holes. You expected much but look how little it turns out to be.' It's as if he saw wage rises going down the petrol tank.

But he says our real problem isn't inflation. It's spiritual bankruptcy. Troubles get on top of us because the weekend is short on spiritual capital. 'While each of you is busy with his own house, the Lord's house remains a ruin.'

A nice house isn't the same as a real home. When spiritual life falls to ruin, home life crumbles too—broken windows in the Lord's house; broken relationships in the nice houses down the street. Without the resources of a weekend word from the Lord to help us cope with stress at work and tension at home, we experience what the prophet meant: 'You expected much, but it turns out to be so little.' We expect much of home life, but without the Lord we have so little of the love, faithfulness and forgiveness we need to carry us through together.

But let me give you a weekend word of hope.

Ruth Carter, sister of the former US President, who had his own Gulf crisis you remember, was on a flight home when the man next to her got talking. He was a millionaire and soon suggested a weekend together.

'No.'

'I bet you've never gone off with a millionaire'

'I haven't.'

'Are you involved with a man?'

'Yes.'

'Are you having an affair with him?'

'No.'

'Then who is he? What's he offering you?'

'His name is Jesus Christ,' she said. 'Jesus offers me not just a weekend but a lifetime, and after that, an eternity. He offers it to you too.'

Ruth returned home to her husband; the spiritually bankrupt millionaire returned to his wife, family, and church. He began to rebuild his life and home upon Christ. He got his weekends sorted out.

3

A Social Worker's Nightmare

The Dream Amidst the Nightmare

Daydreaming can be fun. It can also be foolish. We do it for all sorts of reasons, but usually so that we can run away from hard, present reality. If the going is to be tough for us yet again, how much nicer to dream up something and to slip away into a world of escape. Joseph, Jacob's son, tried it and no wonder, for he was a sensitive misfit in a dreadfully divided family, where the hatreds and jealousies of bully boys at home almost destroyed him.

Then God intervenes and in his sovereign way gets through into the troubled sleep of this young man.

> Joseph, a young man of seventeen, was tending the flocks with his brothers, the sons of Bilhah and Zilpah, his father's wives, and he brought their father a bad report about them. Now Israel loved Joseph more than any of his other sons because he had been born to him in his old age: and he made a richly ornamented robe for him. When his brothers saw that their father loved him more than any of them, they hated him and could not speak a kind word to him.
>
> Joseph had a dream and when he told it to his brothers they hated him all the more. He said to them 'Listen to this dream I had: we were binding sheaves of corn out in the field when suddenly my sheaf rose and stood upright, while your sheaves gathered round mine and bowed down to it.' His brothers said to him 'Do you

intend to rule over us? Will you actually reign over us?'
And they hated him all the more because of his dream
and what he had said...

Gen. 37: 2–8

How Joseph would understand our temptation to
daydream. His case history is a social worker's nightmare.
His father had picked up four wives, his own mother was
now dead. Of his ten older brothers one was incestuous;
two were violent. His father treated him favourably because
he was bright, boosting Joseph's ego and making him feel
superior. As a result, he split on his brothers and they put
him down. Any one would want to dream their way out of
such a conflict situation.

The message of the Joseph story is that God can rescue
us in the most surprising way. This incident shows us that
God, the director behind the scenes, helped Joseph, the
actor on stage. As he trained Joseph to work with him, we
see a lonely human life strengthened and redirected. Part of
Joseph's future under God was to see his own family rescued
and reconciled and it all began when God met him.

Mind you, he didn't communicate that clearly at first.
When he told them at breakfast he was going to be promoted
above them all one day, they must have wanted to throw
their cereal at him. But God always has to deal with our
pride, even after he blesses us. God had great things for him
and he can have them for us too. But he has to deal with that
old day dream image of self first. Joseph still swaggered
a little in his coat of many colours. He is to lose it as he is
plunged down into the depths. But God was there too, as he
can be with you today. It depends on whether we want him
or just the daydreams.

The Pit

We all know what it means to be up in the clouds one day
and right down in the pit the next. High hopes dismally
dashed. For Joseph, it was the hatreds of family in-fighting
that threatened to put an end to his dreams. Who knows
what threatens to fling us into a pit of despondency today?
But God brought Joseph through that kind of darkness.
'You intended to harm me', he said in later years, 'but God

intended it for good'. God intended to train him for a life of responsible leadership.

> Now his brothers had gone to graze his father's flocks near Shechem and Israel said to Joseph…'Go and see if all is well with your brothers and bring back word to me.' ….So Joseph went after his brothers and found them near Goshen. But they saw him at a distance and before he reached them, they plotted to kill him. 'Here comes that dreamer' they said to each other. 'Let's kill him and throw him into one of those cisterns and say that a ferocious animal devoured him. Then we'll see what comes of his dreams.' When Reuben heard this, he tried to rescue him. 'Let's not take his life' he said. 'Throw him into this cistern here, but don't lay a hand on him.'
>
> So when Joseph came they stripped him of his robe—the richly ornamented robe he was wearing—and threw him into the cistern.
>
> Gen. 37: 12–24

First, a challenge. Let's not plot how to put down someone else. What makes us do it? Provocation, jealousy, opportunity. They were all there when the brothers spotted Joseph in the distance. That blessed trendy gear of his—the symbol of unfair privilege—it gave him away a mile off. They suspected he'd come to inform on them again. The memory of those high and mighty dreams stung them. If it wasn't for the eldest brother's intervention, they'd have killed him. It's better to listen to wiser counsel when we're in the business of putting others down.

But there's another challenge here. How will I react if it's me who gets the pit experience? It gets even worse for Joseph. When the brothers did a deal with some Arab transport workers, he was swept into an even darker abyss—he became foreign slave labour.

Perhaps your dreams have ended in a pit of despair. Redundancy, the break up of your family unit, the bewilderment of multiracial life, recurring disappointments. You would have understood if Joseph had been the one to show hatred, revenge, self pity at the mad nonsense of what they were doing to him. Self pity can easily put us all into a pit of our own making. If there is such a type as a 'moaning Minnie', Joseph was a candidate.

But do you know, when next we see him there's not a trace of it. Nor is there a sign of that 'image' of his. His problems were not over, but he was different. Where men tried to harm him, God overruled for his good. He dealt with his problem of self-centredness and trained him to be a true leader and a public servant. Out of the dark soil grew the graceful plant of humility. In those bleak hours before God, the vain, stuck up Joseph died. I have a hunch that in that pit, which must have seemed like a death cell, Joseph remembered the stories of how God had taught old grandfather Isaac that proud self must die if God is to live his life in us. When he re-emerges in the story, he is a new man, a man of God, a man 'in charge' of himself and so later trusted to take charge of others.

When you feel like an absolute nobody and there's nobody to trust, will you trust in God? In the place of bitterness, can we learn to live by the conviction that if we belong to Him, he is still with us, that his standards are the ones to be kept, that he can work everything together for good, even when we are tempted to ask, 'What is the point?'

We never know from what pit he can rescue us. I knew a guy who was an art student. He had started on soft drugs and was slumped one night in a tankard of meaninglessness at his local. 'You need to talk to the Christians,' said a sarcastic friend. And he did. God met him and made a new man of him in Christ—and of his sarcastic friend. Then he began to pray for his father, mother, and sister. One by one, they too came out of meaningless living and are on course to learn more of God's plan for their lives.

A Husband's Neglect?

This incident from the life of Joseph is a common enough scene on any late night television screen. Here we have a young man of striking physique and exceptional ability. The favourite to get on. Eventually he gets the top job. A top dog in a top establishment. Then the affair. Not the office secretary for him, but the Boss's wife—eager for a fling. For her, a younger man in his prime and the ego boosting feeling that she is still wanted. But what about the top marriage— that is—hers? It was thought she had landed a prize when she got that husband of hers. What went wrong for the boss's wife?

> Now Joseph had been taken down to Egypt. Potiphar, an Egyptian who was captain of the guard, bought him from the Ishmaelites who had taken him there. The Lord was with Joseph and he prospered and he lived in the house of his Egyptian master. When his master saw that the Lord was with him and gave him success in everything he did, Joseph found favour in his eyes and became his attendant. Potiphar put him in charge of his household, and he entrusted to his charge everything he owned.... he left in Joseph's care everything he had, with Joseph in charge he did not concern himself with anything except the food he ate.
>
> Now Joseph was well built and handsome and after a while his master's wife took notice of Joseph and said, 'Come to bed with me.'
>
> Gen. 39: 1–4, 6–7

What a typical affair could have emerged from this story. It partly did, except the young man didn't play—not that game. She was picking on the wrong guy. Joseph was in charge, not only of his job, but of himself.

What happened to the marriage of this captain of the King's guard? The story strongly suggests the husband needed to be told a thing or two. It looks as if the conduct of his wife may have been as much a response to Potiphar's neglect of her as Joseph's availability. 'He had no concern in the house but the food that he ate'. It's a case of taking his partner for granted. I'm not trying to provide the woman with a 'How can you blame her?' excuse. I'm pointing out that the Bible gives me, the husband, primary responsibility for the health of my marriage.

So, my question to Captain Potiphar is this: What became of all that extra time you gained for yourself through Joseph's powers of administration? It eased the pressure. Life was a lot less hectic. More time for wife and home. Just at the right time too, when promotion prospects have peaked and the unsettling influence of the mid life crisis lies ahead. What a priceless opportunity to be able to have all those hours to put back into your marriage, to rediscover each other and gain rapport with the woman you used to take on day trips down the Nile.

But it didn't work out that way. It seems your wife became little more than the provider of your meals. No wonder we see the flirting eye, the almost vindictive desire to give herself to someone else, just so she might be noticed. It's the way the women feel in John Wain's *A Travelling Woman*.

It's easy to forget, or never grasp, the first principle of marriage as God intended it. We are to give it first place after our relationship to God himself. Marriage that is commitment for life demands that, and will never yield its thrilling best without it. But so often the company, the practice, the sport, the club, even the church committee can fill our lives at the expense of our closest partner.

For some it ends in drag repetitiveness, self depreciation, lacklustre lives, depressed days, and a 'dead' marriage. For Potiphar's wife it led to the fantasy escape of illicit romance. And it looks as if Potiphar asked for it.

Temptation At The Top

One of the surprises of the television series 'Superstars', at least to the casual fan, was the high level of all round fitness of men who were famous for one particular sport. What we notice about Joseph is God has been training him for all round moral fitness, so when particular temptation pressures him, his resources are sound. He wins under pressure. What he appeared to be in public, he was in private. His reasons for saying no, show he is consistent through and through. No double standards. That is one of the reasons why the Bible lifts the veil off this bedroom scene.

> Now Joseph was well built and handsome and after a while his master's wife took notice of Joseph and said, 'Come to bed with me.' But he refused. 'With me in charge,' he told her, 'my master does not concern himself with anything in the house; everything he owns he has entrusted to my care. No one is greater in this house than I am. My master has withheld nothing from me except you, because you are his wife. How could I do such a wicked thing and sin against God?' And though she spoke to Joseph day after day, he refused to go to bed with her or even to be with her.
>
> Gen. 39: 6–9

Here he is, face to face, woman to man enticement. Are principled convictions any help in the rush of a moment like this? The first brake he applies is this. 'I'm in charge here and your husband entrusted everything to my care'. Wouldn't it have been easy to have found an excuse for saying yes? 'Well, I'm under no check here. No one will find out. Why not?' God's way leaves no room for the so-called eleventh commandment—'Thou shalt not be found out.' Secret opportunity is not a higher law than right or wrong. If a thing is wrong, it is wrong.

His second brake shows how his old image of self importance had been overcome. 'No one at work here is above me.' This could have been the spoilt boy's licence for lust. The meteoric rise to the top can feed vast hidden vanities. How reassuring therefore, to hear him say that the more power he had been given, the greater reason he sees for not using it wrongly for himself. Truly the Lord was with him. Such a man does not need to cover up, but neither does he fear an enquiry. His life was open to God, so he could do the confidential things as if they were in the full light of open government. It was, after all, government that God was training him for.

But for the moment the urgent task was how to govern himself. So he has something else to say. 'Potiphar has withheld nothing from me except yourself, because you are his wife.' Marriage is marriage and it is a fence over which he refused to climb. We may feel cosy and private here; it would be nice to put on some music and have a drink. But marriage is greater than either of us and God has defined its exclusiveness. 'How could I do this great wickedness and sin against God?' For Joseph, sin was offensive to God and no way could he regard this as just a passing and passionate affair.

Integrity Tested

In future years Joseph was to reach the highest political office and to originate the first massive international famine relief programme. But—feet in shackles, neck in irons— suffering and injustice crossed his path to eminence. And mainly because of the fury of a woman scorned.

> One day he went into the house to attend to his duties, and none of the household servants were inside. She caught him by his cloak and said 'Come to bed with me!' But he left his cloak in her hand and ran out of the house...She kept his cloak beside her until his master came home. Then she told him this story: 'That Hebrew slave you brought us came to me to make sport of me. But as soon as I screamed for help, he left his cloak beside me and ran out.' When his master heard this story...he burned with anger. Joseph's master took him and put him in prison...But while Joseph was there in the prison the Lord was with him.
>
> Gen. 39: 11–21

Earlier, we watched Joseph give his decisive no. He might well have thought she had got the message. Not so. The refusal to accept a no tells us a lot about the nature of moral battles. They are rarely won in a day. 'She spoke to Joseph day after day.'

Joseph's moment of truth came with the next move. Talk turned into touch—a sudden switch to the physical. 'She took hold of him and said, "Lie with me here."' It's John Wain's Ruth leading George upstairs by the hand; Alice trapping young Joe Lampton in *Room at the Top*: willing but soon disillusioned parties.

The contrast between them and Joseph is explicitly captured in Rembrandt's etching of the incident. For Joseph it was neck or nothing. And because of his understanding of what God wants marriage to be, it was nothing. 'Woe betide that man,' says Goethe, 'who tries to work out his principles in times of crisis.'

In our day, everything is forever open to question. We're obsessed with pros and cons. 'Thou shalt not be certain of anything' is a Bertrand Russell ditty echoed on a thousand guitars.

Uncertainty was no help to honest Joseph, and it's the Bible that gives us certainty here. Had Joseph toyed with the marriage therapy idea that some partners need affairs to help restore a flagging marriage, this case could well have landed up with a solicitor. Joseph had got hold of the Creator's absolute. This meant he had to snatch himself away, his coat still in her grasp. That's the second he'd lost. With a touch of humour that Joseph must have needed by now, Matthew Henry says, 'Better to lose a good coat than a good conscience.'

We may smile. But this is not the blushing exit of a shy adolescent. Joseph, soon unjustly imprisoned, would be the dominant figure among hard-bitten prisoners in a detention block. He is actually being tough at the toughest point—with himself and his own body. One of the qualifying things he later took with him to high office was that gracious blessing of God—a clear conscience.

And marriage? Well, there was no lovely lady waiting in the wings yet awhile. But Joseph was saving himself for something and someone far better. The Bible has no doubt about it:

> Rejoice in the wife of your youth,
> May her breasts satisfy you at all times;
> Be captivated always by her love.
> Why be captivated, my son,
>   with another man's wife?'
>
> Prov. 5: 18–20

4

A Bad Conscience

Conscience Suppressed

'Conscience,' said an old Red Indian Chief, 'is a sharp three cornered thing inside me. When I do wrong it turns round and hurts me. But when I keep on deliberately doing wrong it will turn round so much that the corners wear off and it fails to hurt me like it did before.'

The Joseph story should be required reading for any of us who have played the dangerous game of trying to rub the edge off conscience. Joseph's brothers had been at it for twenty years. By then they must have thought they had got away with the perfect crime. Their conscience was dulled. But their deceitful actions all those years ago had left the family in a sorry mess. They lived under a shadow. And when famine struck, God began to intervene to reactivate and sharpen up that three cornered thing. Their conscience was reawakened.

> When Jacob learned that there was corn in Egypt, he said to his sons, 'Why do you just keep looking at each other? I have heard that there is corn in Egypt. Go down there and buy some for us, so that we may live and not die'...But Jacob did not send Benjamin, Joseph's brother, with the others, because he was afraid that harm might come to him.
>
> Gen. 42: 1-2, 4

This family had done itself awful harm already. You can understand a father wanting to keep his youngest son out of harm's way when one of his other sons—Joseph—had disappeared without trace. It was twenty years since the ten brothers had massively deceived their father Jacob that Joseph was dead. A shadow of suspicion and fear still hung over them all.

How easily we can harm each other, and then our own consciences, by refusing to mend the damage. What makes the best of us get our own back and down someone else? Provocation? Resentment? Jealousy? Opportunity?

All these factors were present when the brothers ripped off Joseph's 'technicoloured dreamcoat'. It symbolized all those high and mighty dreams of his. How they hated him. The last they had seen of him was as the Arab traders took him off to Egypt and they had shared out the cash they'd got for selling him—twenty pieces of silver. They had long since suppressed any qualms of conscience.

Or had they? Famine began to trouble the home. One day Jacob got the family together. 'Listen, I've got some good news. There's corn down in Egypt. Go, get some.' They all froze and cast furtive glances at each other. Have you known the kind of thing that was happening? You are standing in a group. Suddenly something is said that makes the years catch up with you and you wish the floor would swallow you up. Conscience awakes and stabs at you.

Jacob sensed the atmosphere. 'Why do you just keep looking at each other like that?' They were soon to discover there is no cover up with God. The Bible is perfectly confident about it. 'Behold your sin will find you out.'

Little did those brothers know, as they went to Egypt to allay their pangs of hunger, they would have to face another urgency—the pangs of conscience. For the famine was to lead them to Joseph. And God used Joseph to mend the harm they'd all suffered. That involved mending broken relationships—with him and with each other.

Conscience and Hunger

Even Bob Geldof could learn a thing or two from Joseph's live aid programme of famine relief. Since famine rarely affected Egypt and Palestine simultaneously, this one we're reading about clearly was no ordinary one. It went on for seven years. Joseph's God-given foresight and administrative integrity and resolute fairness saved a whole generation in the Middle East. The Joseph story focuses on one sample family rescued from starvation. Yet the story's main point is summed up in the words of Jesus—'man cannot live by bread alone.'

We in the western world certainly have enough bread to live on; but have we enough to live for?

> Now Joseph was the governor of the land, the one who sold corn to all its people. So when Joseph's brothers arrived, they bowed down to him with their faces to the ground. As soon as Joseph saw his brothers, he recognised them, but he pretended to be a stranger and spoke harshly to them. 'Where do you come from? ' he asked.
>
> 'From the land of Canaan' they replied, ' to buy food.'
>
> Although Joseph recognized his brothers, they did not recognize him. Then he remembered his dreams about them.
>
> Gen. 42: 6–9a

Here we have ten hungry men bent on getting food to survive. They were to get it in abundance, thanks to Joseph. But when they turned up in the queue for corn they failed to recognize that this man in authority was their brother. His dress, language, status, the passing years combined to blind them to his real identity. It meant the only one who could meet their needs was the one they had all wronged so terribly. And he recognised them instantly. As they bowed low to him, Joseph saw at last the destiny God had long prepared for him. He had already been given a dress rehearsal of this in that teenage dream and call of God to high office. Their jealousy then had almost destroyed him. And now they were literally at his mercy, though they didn't know it.

Would he now destroy them because they had tried to destroy him? Would it be revenge at the hand of an Eastern despot? Or would it be reconciliation? Would he just give them food to have enough to live on? Or would he deal with the deep burden of wrong that shadowed the life of this family and give them all something greater to live for?

Later in the story they feast and drink freely with this stranger. But a good meal cannot silence a troubled conscience. Joseph's ultimate aim was more than easing their hunger. Their need was also to face their wrong and to know that the one who they thought was dead was alive and wanted them to know his forgiveness. It's a moving human story, all the more so because it is fertile with reminders of God's way with us, and the way Jesus the Risen Saviour deals with sinful people.

We see Joseph confront their consciences and then win them by his love. He unravels the knots of deceit in this family, shows how the past can be forgiven, how they can know right relationships, and right behaviour.

Conscience and Cover Up

In our heart of hearts, I suppose we all know it is foolish to cover up. Evasion and conspiracy of silence over wrong doing, rather than owning up and aiming for honest and peaceful relationships at home, is short-sighted. Cover up builds up a log jam for the future. It builds up pressure for uncontrollable explosions. And it's even worse when the wronged party knows you're guilty. Joseph knew. His brothers don't know he knows. They don't even know he is alive.

It's a bit too much like the state of play between man and God to be comfortable, don't you think?

> [Joseph] said to them 'You are spies!' 'No, my Lord' they answered. 'Your servants have come to buy food...Your servants are honest men, not spies.'
>
> 'No!' he said. 'You have come to see where our land is unprotected'.
>
> But they replied, 'Your servants were twelve brothers, the sons of one man who lives in the land of Canaan. The youngest is now with our father, and one is no more...
>
> Joseph said to them...'If you are honest men, let one of your brothers stay here in prison, while the rest of you go and take corn back for your starving households. But you must bring your youngest brother to me, so that your words may be verified and that you may not die.'
>
> Gen. 42: 9b-13, 19–20

What is Joseph up to here? He reminds me of a great chess player. He's beginning to make his moves with a patient eye for his eventual aim. He is making these men face themselves and their failures, in preparation for facing him and then his forgiveness. They have refused, up till now, to acknowledge that they have been living an enormous lie.

Under Joseph's interrogation, they claim to be honest men.

'Come off it' thought Joseph. Honest? For all those years they had kept their father in a state of needless and hopeless grief. They had heard his sighs, watched him thinking the worst, head in hands—as we see people driven to distraction when their child goes missing. Just one word from them and he'd have been a different man. And they'd have been different men. You know how easy it is to go out to work today under a cloud, when a 'sorry' or a thoughtful action or an explanation would make all the difference to the day.

Then, after repeated questioning, these hardened but now alarmed men, (spying was a capital offence), give the most ironic reply in the whole Bible.

'Your servants were twelve brothers, but one is no more'. Far from being 'no more', he is there, knowing all about them, able to judge them, help them and yet until he makes himself known to them, they cannot see him for who he is. Again, it's uncannily like what man says of God—I once read a book called *God is no more*.

How can God's holy but invisible existence and man's clever but guilty evasiveness be brought together? Well, the conscience is a starting point and Joseph works on it. To ask why man cannot find God is like asking why a criminal cannot find a policeman. Does he really want to? A conscience matter perhaps?

Conscience Stricken

Now we watch a family that has done itself no end of self inflicted harm, begin the road back to an honest togetherness. What started it was the feeling that some sort of retribution was catching up with them for their callousness and deception. But through it all we are given a peep into the compassionate heart of God as he prods these people to turn to each other and to him, instead of turning against and away from each other and from him.

> They said to one another, 'Surely we are being punished because of our brother. We saw how distressed he was when he pleaded with us for his life, but we would not listen; that's why this distress has come upon us.'
>
> Reuben replied, 'Didn't I tell you not to sin against the boy? But you wouldn't listen! Now we must give an accounting for his blood.'
>
> They did not realize that Joseph could understand them, since he was using an interpreter.
>
> He turned away from them and began to weep...
>
> Gen. 42: 21–4

There is a severe mercy about the goodness of God which is for our good. It's staggering how insensitive we can be to the suffering we put others through—until it begins to happen to us. Beneath the hard exterior of these men was something to be tapped: a submerged awareness that they were deeply in the wrong. Joseph becomes God's instrument to break into their self defence.

Notice first the severity of the means to arouse dulled consciences. They were all cast into prison for a while—a taste of their own medicine. They see Simeon bound as a hostage. Their own misdeeds were re-enacted before their eyes.

At last, and suddenly, the past catches up with them. It's as if it all happened yesterday—though a full twenty years had passed. Everything is replayed on the screen of their memories: at last they are shocked at their refusal to listen to their brother's distress cries. In a typical family 'scene' accusations begin to fly. Reuben can't resist saying 'Didn't I warn you? If you'd listened to me we wouldn't ever have got into this mess.'

What delivered the body blow was the way they were called on to verify the truth of their claims. 'That man' insisted on testing their honesty by demanding young Benjamin. That, they knew, would finish their father. He'd go through all the old anguish again. It all re-emphasized how dishonest they had been. But at least now, they begin to identify and sympathize with the suffering they had brought on their brother and especially their father.

But did you notice in the Genesis passage the thing they failed to see? There is a goodness and mercy following them in the midst of the severity. Joseph had overheard and understood all this family self torture. And he turns aside and hides his tears. Joseph loves them, in spite of it all. It is the goodness of God that leads us to repentance.

God and the Conscience—Facing Up to It at Last

'Man cannot live by bread alone.' Jesus said these words when he himself was hungry in the desert. We need no clearer illustration of their truth than the sight of Joseph's brothers *en route* for home, with corn sacks full, but hearts heavy. Thankfully their hunger had been met from Joseph's granaries—an example where food mountains can be put to good use. But a bitter family row loomed ahead and they dreaded it, because it was all their fault.

I suppose you know the feeling. Deep freeze full, plenty on the table, but it's been nothing but arguing for years.

> Joseph gave orders to fill their bags with corn, to put each man's silver back in his sack, and to give them provisions for their journey…At the place where they stopped for the night one of them opened his sack to get feed for his donkey, and he saw his silver in the mouth of his sack…Their hearts sank and they turned to each other trembling and said, 'What is this that God has done to us?'
>
> Gen. 42: 25–8

Better late than never, but these men had left it an awful long time before they now turn to each other. Open to God at last, they now begin to talk about the way he was pursuing them like the hound of heaven. 'What is this that God has done to us?'

Why did their hearts sink on discovering the silver? If you had bought ten pounds of goods and then discovered you'd been given the ten pounds back as well, would your heart sink? But for these men, that Egyptian silver gets to their consciences, because twenty pieces of silver had sold Joseph into Egypt.

This is the point where they begin to take seriously the fact that their lives are under the eye of God, and is the point where things begin to mend. At last they have stopped turning God off like we turn off the radio.

A missionary surgeon, Paul Brand, tells how he invented a substitute nerve to protect leprosy patients. A very loud painful signal would sound to warn the patient his damaged, unfeeling fingers were in danger. He found the signal had to be put out of the patient's reach. 'If people really wished to do something dangerous, they would switch off the signal and then do what they had in mind to do.'

At last Joseph's brothers had stopped the dangerous game of turning off the signals of conscience. It was to lead back to honesty, repentance and, above all, reconciliation with their father and a living ruler called Joseph who forgave them from the heart. When Joseph made himself known and they realized he was alive, they must have felt like the stricken disciples on meeting the risen Jesus. When Joseph welcomed them, and they received his embrace, their lives were transformed.

It is little wonder Christians see in Joseph someone who foreshadows so much the suffering and risen Saviour whose name is Jesus. He it is who sets our conscience free.

Let our prayer forever be in those words of praise from Isaac Watts, perhaps the greatest of our hymn writers:

> Jesus my great high priest
> Offered his blood and died.
> My guilty conscience seeks
> No sacrifice besides.
> His powerful blood did once atone
> And now it pleads before the throne.
>
> Great prophet of my God
> My tongue would bless thy name.
> By thee the joyful news
> Of our salvation came—
> The joyful news of sins forgiven
> Of hell subdued and peace with heaven.

5

Accountable to Conscience

Has it ever struck you that there is a preacher everyone in the world has heard, including you? A universal voice heard by every generation since the creation of man. He is no respecter of persons. All men are accountable to him. No locked door can keep him out of prison cell or private apartment. He has access into the White House and the Kremlin. He is the last barrier, the slender hope man has that he will not make a destructive mess of everything.

The power of this preacher can be overwhelming. Some have resorted to suicide to try and silence him. Murderers have been constrained to confess. He may have interrupted the course of your life. There you were, looking all composed, when suddenly something was said that turned you hot and cold. Your past caught up with you. The preacher's stabbing voice had spoken. And somehow, you knew he spoke the truth.

His name we know. It's conscience.

How can a man have a good, clear conscience?

Strictly speaking, it is misleading to talk of a good or bad conscience. Our conscience is not good or bad. What conscience does is to pronounce an approving or a disapproving judgement on me. I feel good or bad as I obey or disobey its voice. This tells us something remarkable about conscience, to which the meaning of the word itself gives us a clue. Conscience means 'a knowing together with' someone or something else. Who or what is that someone or something?

According to the Bible, 'God has set eternity in the heart of man' so that, through his conscience, man knows 'together with'—that is, he is conscious of a moral law that is over and above his own will. We are all familiar with this. My conscience somehow stands apart from me. It is as if the 'I' of conscience takes a position outside of 'me', observes me and makes a judgement on me—and it doesn't have to ask my permission to do so. Conscience protests if I do wrong.

But, of course, conscience can pronounce opposing judgements in different people. Does that mean conscience is just the product of different upbringing, religious prejudice, education, so that conscience has a natural origin?

Not at all. To see that, we must distinguish between the form and the content of conscience. It takes the form of a judgement seat, which tells a man he ought to do what he believes to be right. Conscience therefore is not a law maker. It's there to pass judgement on the person who has to obey. As soon as we are clear about that, we can see that conscience everywhere remains constant in one thing—it is an independent authoritative judgement seat within us.

But what about the different judgements conscience pronounces? This derives chiefly from two things. Firstly, it is according to the knowledge or lack of knowledge of the law of God that the individual possesses. Secondly, all sorts of other factors in his background influence its judgement.

The biblical teaching on the creation of man and his fall into sin explains the constant and the variation. That conscience sticks to its role as a judgement seat testifies to the fact God is our Lawgiver and will one day be our Judge. But, equally, the fact that the judgement of conscience varies in one another demonstrates the confusing effects of our fall into sin, and the deficient knowledge of the law of God that has resulted. Conscience is like a faulty radio receiver. Its reception is faint; the voice is subject to distortion and to interference from other sources; it cannot be tuned in properly.

So, too, the Bible explains that the root cause of the inadequacy of conscience is this contact problem between man and God. When contact is restored and the voice of

God's law is heard clearly, the standards by which the conscience judges is restored too. And when that happens, the question, how can I have a good conscience? becomes an urgent one. It becomes synonymous with the question, how can I have a right relationship with God?

6

A Permissive Society

Most of us in the Western world live in a society which has got one pervading ideology—a kind of unofficial secular religion. We give it various names. Some call it the compassionate society, others the permissive society, and others 'the freedom-to-choose' society.

This idea is behind it all, says James Packer. The purpose of the community or the state is to extend the range of choices open to the individual—you and me. Included within that, is the freedom to pursue our own personal morality.

We have replaced God's absolutes, his commands concerning right and wrong with, ironically, our own absolute: the idea that the individual should be free to live as he prefers. His morals are his own business. So we are in difficulty over defining what is right and wrong. A student newspaper in the heady days when these ideas were winning ground wrote: 'Students must be given moral freedom to make their own decisions to act as they choose. No one has the right to tell anyone how they should behave.'

The problem with such anarchic banners is this: that sort of individual self interest pursued to its conclusion, begins to undermine the society of which we are a part.

Our predominant community ideal tries to combine the freedom of permissiveness—which I would define as unrestrained self love—with the obligation of compassion. Permissiveness says we have the right to make all sorts of disastrous moral choices in the name of freedom. Compassion is then supposed to step in to support us through the damaging consequences of those choices.

That produces a long term problem, which is already in evidence. How can self interest, or freedom to do as we want, provide a moral base for a stable and caring community? What happens is that permissiveness destroys true compassion because it eats away at its foundations. Society is the sum of all its parts. If a growing percentage of its parts are acting only out of self interest—what suits me—then the whole caring structure starts to crack.

I heard about three people collecting for the blind in the foyer of a London cinema. The cinema was showing two films, a family film and a film of sex and violence, which according to the prevailing consensus does the community no harm. Almost everyone coming out of the family film gave the collectors a donation for the blind. Only one person coming out of a packed sex and violence film gave the collectors anything. That is an on the spot reflection of how permissiveness erodes compassion. It debases our nature so we treat people and other people's problems with an increasing indifference.

The self love that is at the root of our moral free-for-all inevitably plays havoc with relationships. Life means relationships. If we cannot forge forgiving long-term relationships, we are left as lonely islands. That's not life for anyone. It becomes a burden and a meaningless misery. God's commands have to do with relationships. Get our relationships right and life can be a joy. Get our relationship with God right and we have found the source of personal and social wisdom.

Around two thousand years ago, the wise men went seeking Jesus. Wise men still do, says a car sticker. It's the beginning of wisdom.

7

The Crime Rate

On opening my wallet the other day I found all my money had been stolen—and my bank card. Help! I phoned the bank. Someone had already tried to use my card but, thankfully, it had been chewed up.

Why do I tell you this? Earlier that week the latest annual crime figures had come out. I sighed at yet another rise in crime. But because it didn't touch me personally, it was just another set of statistics. But that Friday morning, I got a little personal taste of what you must feel like if you've been victim of more serious crime.

How do we beat it? Despite the good ideas we hear at the party conferences, few face the root cause of our moral slide—our fallen human nature. But can human nature be changed? A nineteen year old once told me how he went to a sweet shop and told the astonished proprietor that years before he had stolen some liquorice. He now wanted to pay. What caused the change? He'd begun to read the Bible, became a Christian, and Jesus had shown him he must be honest and not steal. I recently watched a smartly dressed child of five fill his pockets with sweets in a store and slip outside to his conniving parents. Soon that hand will be in wallets, unless there is a real change of heart there too.

You'll find evidence of that change from an NSPCC (National Society for the Prevention of Cruelty to Children) Inspector in the Rhondda Valley in South Wales: 'Homes that I have had under observation for some time, have undergone a complete transformation through the parents having been brought to a better life. In a couple of cases where I thought I would have to prosecute, the conversion of the father in one home and mother in the other means it is no longer necessary.'

That Report is dated 1904, showing how the Welsh Revival transformed many a problem home. The Society's Reports for 1990 are heartbreaking. We've run out of the spiritual power that redeems people. Why? A Liverpool MP put it this way—'we've been raiding the beehive for honey and failing to feed the bees for too long—we can't maintain Christian moral standards because we've stopped feeding ourselves Christian truth.'

That truth gave our country, with all its faults, a name for honesty. It can still show. Someone told a hotel receptionist recently that his phone calls may not have registered on his bill, so how much did he owe? 'Oh you British!' she said, 'You are so honest. This would never happen in my country.' Her country had known little of what we used to call gospel truth, God's truth makes people truthful and trustworthy; where their word is their bond.

But what kind of country are we becoming? All party conferences hold any government responsible for rising crime. Yet no government can govern the hearts of its people. But I'm sure of one thing, the Spirit of Christ gives us power to govern ourselves. He deals with the problem of human nature. Where there is a genuine turning to the Lord and people's lives are transformed by his love and law, the NSPCC sees the change for the better.

What will we see? Our children turned increasingly into crime statistics? In a general turning to Christ, people remember their Creator in the days of their youth, and God spares us such evil days. Moral crisis has often led to spiritual renewal.

Wallets are safer too.

8

God Moves in Strangeways

'God moves in strange ways' read a recent headline. Then I read it again. 'God moves in Strangeways.' Ah—it meant what is now Manchester prison. Some twelve months before, television screens had carried shots of mayhem in Strangeways prison, with prisoners establishing a no-go area on the roof and merrily hurling slates to the floor. It was a twenty-five day wonder, with world wide media coverage. But then it fell out of the news.

Who was picking up the pieces a year later? Prisoners were moved all over the country. Distance put even more strain on marriages, adding to bitterness and anger. The staff too, were deeply wounded and scarred. So, what did the headline mean—God moves in Strangeways?

Well, there was already a hive of Christian activity there before the troubles—twenty-nine services and Bible classes each week. The riot started in the chapel—showing how the rioters used this interest in the gospel services as a cover. But among those moved, post riot, to other jails were some who had genuinely turned to Christ. Their changed lives were making their mark. Hard evidence of that comes from the places they moved to. A policeman in another town said he'd always questioned the work of prison chaplains until 'these lads' arrived from Strangeways. They read their Bibles; their behaviour was better. They told him how the saving power of Jesus had changed them.

Another policeman, from Leamington, described how he had seen a new arrival from Strangeways wash his cell of graffiti and ask for paint to decorate it. He told the policeman Jesus had come into his life and given him a new motivation. It stirred that police officer to seek God himself: 'I never thought a prisoner would make me think seriously about my life', he said.

Then a prison officer said how he'd been watching the chaplains during and after the troubles. 'I saw the calm and peace in your lives, even though you were suffering as much as any of us. I thought, if having faith in Jesus Christ gives them these qualities, then I want to find it too.'

These prisoners and chaplains, police and prison officers, tell the same story: God is at work in Strangeways. The chaplain's wife put a note of encouragement in his Bible, specially relevant at Easter time. It read: 'After the crucifixion comes the resurrection to new life, new beginnings. In the chaos of Strangeways stands Jesus saying, "Don't despair, behold I make all things new. Heaven and earth will pass away, but the Word of God endures for ever." So, hang in there!'

It wasn't easy to hang in there amidst the structural chaos. That went when the building was made new in 1994. But the human chaos? That requires making men new. 'I've realised even more the power of the living Christ to change men into new creations of decency and responsibility' says a chaplain. 'His life-giving power is the one factor which can rehabilitate.'

When that chaplain met one of the dispersed prisoners in Reception recently, the man hugged him and said, 'Before April last year I was not a real Christian; I was on the touch line. But now I'm one of the "Team for Jesus".' In them, at least, the chaos is passing away.

Perhaps the least surprised are the 600 members of the public who wrote to the prison after the riot to assure the Christian team of their prayer support. God moves in strange ways.

9

That F Letter Word

Lots of four letter words are good—hope, care, help, love. But there's the other sort too. Recently the Broadcasting Standards Council published reactions to swearing on radio and television. Eighty-seven percent were caused discomfort by the four letter 'F' word.

It was first used on television by Kenneth Tynan in 1965. Funny and scathing, the force behind *Oh! Calcutta!*, he was into sexual liberation and the freedom to say in public what former standards had kept private. What was he like, this lover of outrage?

I'm not joining the trend to nose out people's private ways in public. But Tynan reveals in his own journal a deep conflict about overturning Christian standards. The Christian testimony of C. S. Lewis, his famous Oxford tutor, probed him all his days, pursuing him like Aslan of Lewis's Narnia stories.

For example, when he read Lewis's *That Hideous Strength*—a space adventure about the fight between good and evil, he wrote: 'Once more the old tug reasserts itself—a tug of genuine war against my recent self. How thrilling Lewis makes goodness seem—how radiant and tangible.' But then, says his biographer, 'C. S. Lewis and sin dissolved and he decided to write an erotic screenplay.'

Anyone who decides to turn away like that from the tug of radiant goodness faces another problem—real guilt before God. Listen to Tynan's private turmoil about this, on reading Lewis's *Problem of Pain*. 'As ever,' he wrote, 'as ever, I respond to his powerful suggestion that guilt and shame are not conditioned by the world in which we live, but are the real apprehensions of the standards obtained in an eternal world'.

That is the man of *Oh! Calcutta!* speaking. Lewis had got under his intellectual skin and laid bare his soul to standards more awesome than any Standards Council. If the eternal world is real, if God is radiant goodness, and if, in spite of it, I prefer a freedom that rejects him, guilt is real too.

The man apparently so free in public to cast off restraints, was in trouble here. In his last illness, he tells us, fear of death made him afraid to sleep. No one is truly free till that fear is taken away.

It comes only when we know our guilt is taken away. And that is exactly what Christ did for us in his death.

In *The Problem of Pain* Lewis commends that truth in these words: 'What are you asking God to do? To wipe away past sins? But he has done so, on Calvary'.

I can't say if Tynan even asked. But if he did, he'd have been just as surprised by the joy of sins forgiven as was Lewis at his conversion. We need fear no evil when Christ's love frees us from guilt. Such love is a four letter word we can't do without.

10

'It's just not cricket'

Test cricket was losing its cool. The brilliant West Indies sides were showing unbeatable world dominance. After the angry battles of the Aussies' tour of the West Indies, there were promises that we'd no longer have to watch the unsporting face of sport. But the old image of 'playing the game' was in decline. That's bad! Cricket is more than a game. After all, isn't life itself is to be played with a straight bat? To break honourable codes of fair play in life is just 'not cricket'.

Sadly, much cricket is now 'not cricket'.

During a One Day Test at Lord's, the television commentator identified the man sitting on the balcony with Ted Dexter, an England cricket selector, as the Reverend Andrew Wingfield Digby—newly appointed chaplain to the England Test team. The selectors are not daft enough to think any team's losing habit will end if a vicar prays about it. The Christian gospel doesn't improve your cricket. But it will help us live life with a straighter bat and play fair with others.

That's where the chaplain comes in. It's a growth industry in sport these days. Dozens of soccer clubs now have them. Perhaps it was the hidden factor behind England winning the Soccer Fair Play Trophy. Are basic issues being faced— that it is estrangement from Christianity that has so badly affected the whole tenor of public life? Playing a selfish game or a dirty game is not just a question of sport.

But if sportsmen are finding an answer in the power of God to that flaw in our nature that causes flare ups on the field, and off it, let's rejoice! Under the pressure of media glare, huge rewards, the lash of tabloid criticism—don't the lads need caring spiritual management?

And as a society—don't we need role models who'll give us more than four letter words at moments of triumph or failure? The club chaplain may be God's man for the hour. In a quiet chat or team talk, where there's no psyching up into hate, some are finding new resources both for playing the game, and for playing the game of life itself. Both become cleaner and more fulfilling than they ever imagined. I'm quoting lots of Christians in sport who have told us so on television. They can have the best influence imaginable on this generation, like the Olympic gold medallist who drew 700 Cambridge students to hear his Christian testimony.

There are many others—a Cambridge University half back, a Neath three quarter, a Newbridge forward, a first division striker, a television sports commentator and so on. They may not have the *Chariots of Fire* impact of Eric Liddell, but they share his priority to honour Christ in life and sport.

The Bible uses many pictures from sport to describe the Christian life: 'Let us run with total commitment the race that is marked out for us, with our eyes fixed on Jesus the author and perfecter of our faith.' He's aptly called the Captain of our Salvation. He's the One who can bring us through life's great Final Test.

What a celebration—when stumps are drawn, the whistle blows, the race ended—to be greeted by him.

11

War and Peace

The Just War

On the First of February 1933—two days after Hitler came to power—a pastor named Bonhoeffer walked into the German Broadcasting Company in Berlin and fell foul of the new dictator. It showed how quickly a nation can be mislead, how difficult it is to stem the tide, and how a just war is sometimes inevitable.

On that February morning, Bonhoeffer gave a broadcast on the concept of the Führer—the leader. He ended with this warning: 'Don't place blind faith in any leader. Such a leader will gradually become the Misleader. Any leader who makes an idol of himself mocks God'. Perhaps Bonhoeffer was thinking of the Bible's teaching about the final dictator—the man of lawlessness who sets himself up in place of God.

As he left the studio, he was told his last sentences had not been broadcast. The microphone had been turned off. The new leader was already the Misleader, silencing opposition at home. In the end, other nations had to stop his aggression. His own people were unable or unwilling to stop him themselves.

In some ways, the 1991 Gulf war against Saddam Hussein repeated the story. Brave souls who sought to resist him at home were silenced. As a classic Misleader he twisted the ideals of millions of young people to his own ends, annexing territory, stirring racial hatred. Complex though the issues are, a consensus of nations ventured on a just war.

When you watch television close ups of casualties it's difficult to find comfort in the idea of the just war. I recall the nights we hid under the stairs when Second World War bombs rained down on Swansea. The idea wasn't much comfort then.

But I'll tell you when it did make sense to me. Just a year or two after the war, I sat in a packed church in my home town to hear Bonhoeffer's friend, Martin Niemöller. He had been in Dachau concentration camp for seven years—his reward for a courageous face to face protest to Hitler. Over-modest about his own efforts, he spoke of the consequences of failing to resist evil men.

'In Germany,' he said, 'they came first for the Communists, and I didn't speak up because I wasn't a Communist. Then they came for the Jews, and I didn't speak up because I wasn't a Jew. Then, the trade unionists, and I didn't speak up because I wasn't a trade unionist. Then, the Catholics, and I didn't speak up because I was a Protestant. Then they came for me, and by that time no one was left to speak up.'

Well, not in Germany. So war was necessary to deliver them and the world. At the end of that war, listening, in my home town, to that German pastor not long out of Dachau, I saw a little of why the dreadful sacrifice of the just war is sometimes necessary. But will it never end?

The Bible has a climactic view of war and history. It is realistic about evil. One day that ultimate Misleader—the man of lawlessness—will arise. His power no human force can stem. But he will be overthrown—by Christ, the Prince of Peace, whose just rule will bring in that long elusive hope—a new world order and a just and lasting peace.

War sharpens our awareness of ultimate realities. People talk of Armageddon—little wonder when we see the night sky lit up by missiles, and Christ speaks of signs in the heavens as a signal of his coming. Let's keep alert and pray.

Dismantling the Soviet System

The dramatic fall of Gorbachev, Boris Yeltsin's courageous climb on to the turret of a tank and the rapid dismantling of the Soviet system was absorbing everyone's attention.

When I watched someone sign his new car registration document, it somehow set me thinking about crumbling Soviet atheism and our western moral crisis. I noticed that our UK document draws a distinction between being a car owner and a car keeper. As far as a car goes, we can be both its owner and keeper. But what about our life? The Christian believes he does not own his life, he holds it on lease from his Creator. He is to be the responsible keeper of the vehicle of personality that God has created.

One of two things follow when we refuse to accept that God owns us. The first is what happened in the Soviet empire—people ended up being owned by tyrants. The root cause of atheistic communism's collapse is that it could only operate by owning its citizens. Such tyranny failed because it tried to operate a false world, a soul-less world, a world of Big Brother's invention and therefore a world that could not work because it denied the basis of human dignity, namely, that the world we live in is God's world, and that denying it does not alter the fact or make it unnecessary to believe it.

We in the West also deny that fact, ironically in the name of freedom, and we're facing the second consequence of turning from God. Our crisis is the collapse of the personal disciplines that are the basis of a free society. It is the Western form of a problem that rejection of a wise, holy, and loving Creator engenders. So we have little to teach the former Soviet empire in ultimate terms. Democracy and the market economy aren't everything. We have them both—and a crisis.

Our rejection expresses itself as humanism, which, at best, is morality without faith. It leans heavily, however, on the Christian basis for democratic responsibility that it has borrowed from the past. Today's humanists live as if we own ourselves, and that means living as though I'm free to run my life as if God is irrelevant. But then the problem in the west becomes increasingly that of how to govern 'us', the people, who received our freedoms under Christian constraints, when democracy was dependent on individuals acting responsibly before God, recognizing that our final reference point for right and wrong was the authority of our Creator Judge. Without that, our social scientists are left with the puzzle of what they call the lack of 'social self control'. Viable democracy cannot coexist with the idea of every man being an independent state, morally his own king.

For then we end up with the western kind of tyranny, that of lawless self interest. It has all the consequent breakdowns of self control in families. Its driving ethos is the survival of the fattest—the fattest bank balance. It shows that both democracy without God and Marxism without God have potential explosions within them. The Soviet regime said God is dead, but millions, at great personal cost, believed 'Christ is risen'. I have stood with some of them deep in the forest as they prayed for a turning of the tide.

Perhaps they have begun to see it now.

Blessed are the Peacemakers

There are times when the sky seems full of peacemakers, as it was when Lord Carrington, Boris Yeltsin, the UN Secretary General, the Northern Ireland Secretary, Secretary of State James Baker, all shuttled to and fro in their attempts to give peace a chance. For a while prospects of peace in many world trouble spots seemed to be possible. Then, in the midst of it all, international peacemaker James Baker commented on the need of personal peace.

James Baker and company grapple with the realities of conflict. Yet, conflict is not just out there, a concern of statesmen. Battles go on inside us, especially when we want something and don't get it. It's in us the problem of peace begins, says professional peacemaker James Baker.

He used to believe power politicians should never admit to personal problems. But that changed when he not only had a personal problem but saw that he was that problem. In seeking the peace of God he found that love for our marriage partner, friends, and God Himself are the most important dimension of life. Baker tells us, 'I really needed to stop trying to play God, and turn the matter over to him.'

Personal peace depends on 'turning the matter over to him'—basic matters, like the whole network of spite, unfairness, conceit that runs in us all. A change in us there is the key to being a peacemaker among others. I don't mean 'being religious'—religion can be a conflict producer of its own. Jesus is more radical than religion. When you become a child of God, he says in one of the Beatitudes, you will begin to share something of God's concern to be a reconciler. 'Blessed are the peacemakers.' None of us can change the world, but each one of us can change the world of just one other person, even now, by being a peacemaker. It has public benefits too.

It showed at a Christian youth Conference at a Northern Ireland University recently. On the platform together were an Orangeman and a former IRA member. Both had been converted to Christ, the latter while a prisoner in the Maze. Nationalism mixed with religion had separated them like concrete walls. But when they turned themselves over to Christ he brought them peace with God and with each other. They demonstrated it. And its public impact was heartening.

A glimpse of peacemaking at home can do the same.

A couple had broken up, and were living in separate apartments in the same house, waiting for the divorce to come through. The man heard the Sunday Morning service on BBC Radio 4. It was about walls of anger in the home that come between people and how Jesus is the door back to God and to each other. This so melted his anger that he knew God was telling him to go and make peace. He went to his estranged wife's room. She too had that programme on, and she too was crying. In Christ they found a reconciler, and the barriers came down.

We can be peace envoys where we are. 'I give my peace to you,' says Christ. If we receive it, like that proud Orangeman, that ex-terrorist, and that angry husband, we can convey it to others.

St Petersburg

Signs that the old Marxist regime was over for good kept on coming out of Russia. When Leningrad reverted to being called St Petersburg it left me ruminating on pre-revolutionary days when the gospel permeated the highest reaches of Russian society.

It might never have changed if a quite phenomenal evangelical movement which occurred in the city before the revolution, had been left to work its way to the moral heart of government. The old guard of privileged nobility saw many of their fellow aristocrats show startling new priorities of social concern. It stemmed from their conversion to Christ. The city buzzed with news of counts, colonels, cabinet members, court princesses meeting for prayer and Bible study.

It all began under the preaching of an English noble, Lord Radstock, a member of the Waldegrave family. Since his conversion to Christ as a young army officer, he had himself turned away from the empty status symbols of London Society. He began to preach, and share his riches with the poor. Eventually, one of the Tzar's Court invited him to St Petersburg. The life-changing power of his preaching amidst the city's jewelled extravagance drew this response from Dostoievsky: 'He performs miracles over human hearts. Those converted are looking for the poor in order to bestow benefits upon them as quickly as possible. They are ready almost to give away their fortunes.'

Here are two examples. A Russian Colonel, the high flyer of the Petersburg circle, owner of vast estates and copper mines in the Urals, knelt like a child and accepted Christ's lordship over his life. With eyes now opened to the needs about him, he began to use his wealth to alleviate it. Count Bobrinsky, a government minister heard Radstock and was thrown into turmoil. Mankind, said Radstock, was lost in sin and there was no possibility of real change, personally or politically, except as individuals found Christ. The Count could not shake off the conviction that this was true, and he yielded, asking Christ to cleanse and remake him. 'I found that Jesus was the key of it all'. Other leaders found so too and the moral heart of a nation could well have changed.

What came of it all? The old regime, threatened by signs of such reformation in its own drawing rooms, throttled it within a decade, only to be swept away itself in 1917.

Yet Radstock's work hasn't died. Many of the flourishing churches in Russia today owe their origin to his witness. For example, one night a distinguished German doctor called Baedeker heard Radstock preach. 'I went in' he says, 'a proud German infidel, and came out a humble, believing disciple of the Lord Jesus Christ.' And for thirty amazing years his life proclaimed his Lord throughout the vast expanse of Russia. Dr Baedeker brought the message of

Christ to every prison in Russia, every convict settlement in Siberia. Tolstoy writes of some of his deeds. Thousands found Christ, and out of those beginnings have come the millions of today.

I happened to meet some people who had heard Lord Radstock preach. The sheer joy of their memories of this servant of God, stirred me to tell his story.

12

Election Day and the Last Day

Would the Prime Minister call the election earlier or later? It kept the media in a fever of conjecture. For long months, democracy ran a high temperature. Having endured the latest trend, pre-election election fever, how much more real election fever could the patient survive without getting delirious.

But constant political debate before democratic elections is no bad thing. 'Democracy' said Winston Churchill, 'is the worst form of government…until you try any other.' Though the verbal violence of electioneering may embarrass us, at least it's the most civilized form of 'civil war' ever devised. The former Eastern Bloc has few doubts that democracy, despite the awesome new problems it has brought them, is to be preferred to the long dark night of oppression they have emerged from. Elections are a day of reckoning—a healthy (if feverish) device that keeps leaders accountable and hopes in democracy high.

Hope we must. But Churchill was right. Even at its best, democracy has a worm in the bud. Every fresh start falters because fallen humanity can't avoid failure. In elections, fallible people judge fallible leaders. It follows that remedies are fallible, often contradictory, always short-lived. Every switch of votes confirms that.

But, these days, hopes are uneasy because of something much more fundamental. What's happening to people?—the raw material of democracy—to you, me and our neighbour in this free society? Responsible freedom is turning into a 'free for all', reducing different strata of society to jungles of strife. There's a shameless crookedness about. Human sin seems to be off the leash, defying restraint, playing havoc with family, honesty, and safety. The power of the vote can't counteract these forces, even though they're now issues at every election. The history of our land shows they only yield, more or less, when I, you, and our neighbour turn back to God and the Christian gospel. Then freedom finds self-discipline in welcoming his commands. Back comes respect for authority too.

When democracy forgets its most famous banner—In God We Trust—it loses its life preserver. In a world gone astray, we can't trust democracy alone. Our problems are vertical before they're horizontal. God calls us first to turn to him if we're to straighten out our lives. Justice and care, in government and people, wither without that. But God also tells us the days of human government itself are numbered. It's too flawed because we're too flawed. So he calls us to prepare for the final reckoning when he'll put things right among us. He has appointed a day when he will judge the secrets of our hearts by Jesus Christ. That day of reckoning delays, its date uncertain. But then, uncertainty over when the election would come didn't cancel out the certainty that it had to come one day.

Wise men prepare for certainties, despite how long they are in coming. I love the prophet Isaiah's unforgettable picture of God's coming rule. Immanuel, God with us, the Prince of Peace will take the Government upon his shoulders. Might and right unite in him. He both judges evil and gives just decisions for the destitute. The strong no longer prey upon the weak, and even the toddler is free from harm. The earth will be filled with the knowledge of the Lord. His government and peace will never end. The fever is over once and for all.

13

Manifesto for Mankind

> Then Jesus said to them, 'These are my words which
> I spoke to you, while I was still with you, that everything
> written about me in the law of Moses and the prophets
> and the psalms, must be fulfilled.
>
> Luke 24: 44

We live in a world that is disillusioned with words. Are
words to be trusted any more? There are manifestos
enough—promises abound. But will they be fulfilled?

A manifesto is a public declaration by a sovereign or some
body of people about what is going to be done. You have
not got to question the integrity of such people to say 'Ah.
But how can anyone guarantee their words will be fulfilled?'
Unexpected crises play havoc with such plans. People get
sceptical about words because even the best words of men
do not include the creative power to bring what is said to
pass. No ordinary mortal can guarantee his words must be
fulfilled in everything.

So what are we to make of Jesus' words in Luke 24?
'Everything must be fulfilled that is written about me [in
the Old Testament]...the Christ will suffer and rise again
from the dead on the third day'. The Old Testament is
God's written manifesto declaring beforehand what he
was going to do through sending Jesus into the world. It's
a little bit, though only a little, like the *Radio Times*. Every
week it is written before the planned programme comes to

pass, but the programme God produces, doesn't run the risk of alteration, cancellation, or technical hitches. God's words are both true and creative. In Jesus, everything the manifesto declares has been fulfilled, or will be fulfilled.

Look at some of the reasons why this manifesto, which is neither right, nor left, nor centre, is unique

Jesus, 'the Christ' (v. 46) is radical: more truly radical than any leftist. He says, 'Behold I make all things new.' It's relatively easy for a revolutionary crowd to destabilize a community. It's a different thing to have radical solutions that go to the root cause of our problems. Jesus can radically change us.

Jesus, 'the Christ', is conservative: more so than any rightist. He is fundamental as well as radical. Behind the Hebrew word for truth lies the root idea of stability—his words give reliable foundations. 'He is the same yesterday, today and' not just tomorrow, but 'for ever'. When you say of someone, 'He's always the same, so dependable,' it is to him you go when in need. The Jesus who can radically change us is himself unchangeably the same.

Jesus 'the Christ' is central: more so than any centrist. So central is he that the universe would not exist or continue without him.

Here we are on spaceship earth. How did time and space come to exist? Who put spaceship earth into orbit? The big question, says Sartre, is that something exists rather than nothing exists. A speaker in Hyde Park was once arguing that this world was the product of pure accident and had 'happened' by itself—none should bother to ask who had created it. Suddenly a tomato orbited past his cheek. 'Who threw that?' demanded the orator. 'No one,' said someone from the back of the crowd, 'it threw itself'.

The manifesto declares that the Lord of the universe holds it all together too. 'In him we live and move and have our being.' Back in the 1950's, I heard George Kennan, the illustrious American, speak to our history seminar in University College, Swansea. Students were then disturbed at the early hydrogen bomb tests. 'What is your expectation for the future?' a student asked. 'Though I fear for the future' he replied, 'I also believe one of the reassuring truths of the

Bible is that in Christ all things cohere and hang together. He is the lynchpin of the universe.'

This central, fundamental, radical figure—'the Christ'—has a perfect public image. It needs no varnishing for the media. He is 'the image of the invisible God' and 'full of grace and truth'. Our delight is to portray him as he is. He cannot be improved upon. Much television theology has tarnished our understanding. The wife of one of our public leaders was once asked, 'Don't you think your husband needs to change his image?' 'I'm mad about him as he is', was her valiant reply. I get properly mad with those who take philosophical axes and hack away at the one perfect public image this world has seen—don't you?

But though Jesus, 'the Christ' is so far above us, he is a leader who is never remote from the common man. 'The common people heard him gladly.' Some leaders lack compassion and the common touch; 'he is a man of sorrows and acquainted with grief.' He had not the slightest pompous concern for his own image when he came among us as a servant of others.

He is not intimidated, though, by the high and mighty. He cannot be dismissed. No pressure group can ever get him to deviate from the justice of God. No trendy revisionist or power bloc can topple him, for he is King of kings and Lord of lords. He shall reign for ever. His government shall not fall and of his kingdom there shall be no end.

All that, of course, is in the manifesto—some of it still to be fulfilled, even if it is to come as a new-created spring the other side of a doomsday scenario. One thing we must remember here is that God has also a secret manifesto (Deut. 29: 29). Most of the future is veiled to us. But God has officially leaked a bit for our encouragement in adversity, a glimpse in advance of the great finale. There is glory to come. We ain't seen nothin' yet.

Jesus, 'the Christ' is also, therefore, Lord of all as well as one of us. In him there is a perfect union of manager and worker. The Creator and Controller of the universe was also outcast and stranger, born at risk in a back garden shed. 'Our God contracted to a span, incomprehensibly made man.'

Why did he come? The answer is in the manifesto. 'These are my words...the Christ will suffer' (v 46). He came as the people's representative to suffer in their place. No other people's representative has represented his people in this way. 'Why should I support your policies?' shouts a heckler at his Member of Parliament. 'What have you ever done for me?' We may understand and sympathize. But men say this about God too. And there they are wrong. Is it nothing to you that he who bore our griefs and carried our sorrows, died, the just in place of we who are unjust, to bring us to God? No people ever had such a wonderful representative as those who go to God through him.

Finally, to the manifesto again. 'The Christ…will rise again the third day' (v. 46). Government leaders come and go. An occasional comeback there may be, but here today, gone tomorrow. But how about his comeback? This leader not only died, he rose again. You cannot read the manifesto and miss that. He said he would rise again and he did. What a foolhardy thing to put in a manifesto, some would say. What an irresponsible thing to do, promising what he could not fulfil. 'But everything written about me must be fulfilled,' he assured his disciples.

And surely enough, not even cold-blooded establishment terrorism, which was what Calvary was on one level, could rip one word of fulfilment from the pages of this manifesto for mankind. 'He rose again on the third day so that repentance and forgiveness of sins should be preached in his name to all nations.'

14

'You Can't Change Human Nature'

Have you heard the story of the tadpole and the frog? The
tadpole swam about in his murky pool, convinced this
was the whole of the existing world. Then, one day, he met
frog.

'I say! Where have you come from?'

'Dry land, actually,' said frog.

'Dry land?' said tadpole, who was a very modern sort.
'Surely there's no such thing. The world I know is as wet as
can be.'

'Oh well, be a sceptic if you wish,' said frog. 'I've just
come from there. It's warm and light up there too. The sun
shines, you know.'

This made tadpole wonder if there was something wrong
with frog. They fell into an argument about how you could
prove there was sun and warmth, and what was 'dry'.

Frog found the argument impossible. In the end, he swam
away saying, 'Unless a tadpole is metamorphosed, he just
can't see or enter the kingdom of the dry.' It left tadpole half
thoughtful, half scornful.

'Does he mean I've got to be changed?'

A while ago a sixth form discussion group, eager tadpoles
swimming about in a sea of modern education, was asked
this question by senior tadpole.

'What one measure would you adopt to help secure peace
in the world this year?' 'Change human nature,' replied one

of the class, frog like. It was thought to be a good answer, indeed astonishing, but not worth discussing, because surely, it wasn't practicable.

'You can't change human nature' we say. True. We can't. If only we could.

But what about Jesus' words, 'What is impossible with men is possible with God'? Jesus himself said unless we experience a God-given change of nature, a spiritual birth as he puts it, we shall never see, or enter, the kingdom of heaven.

Like bright tadpole, people are full of objections to this.

So let's see how a parable can help. It describes two men who were both equally in need of this change, as we all are. One was definitely the religious type, the other definitely the opposite.

> To some who were confident of their own righteousness and looked down on everybody else, Jesus told this parable: 'Two men went up to the temple to pray, one a Pharisee and the other a tax collector. The Pharisee stood up and prayed about himself: `God, I thank you that I am not like other men—robbers, evildoers, adulterers—or even like this tax collector. I fast twice a week and give a tenth of all I get.' 'But the tax collector stood at a distance. He would not even look up to heaven, but beat his breast and said, `God, have mercy on me, a sinner.' 'I tell you that this man, rather than the other, went home justified before God. For everyone who exalts himself will be humbled, and he who humbles himself will be exalted.'
>
> Luke 18: 9–14

By focusing our attention on these two people, Jesus shows us exactly what he means by human nature being changed. He puts it in terms of our relationship to God. By concentrating the issue around two people he is telling us that, in the sight of God, there are only two kinds of people—those whom God rejects and those whom God accepts.

To cross that great divide is the greatest thing in life. It marks the crucial change in human nature. Put another way, it means we become a new person in Christ. It's impossible for us to do, but it is possible for God.

In this parable Jesus shows us firstly, the kind of resistance barriers to change that exist in us. We should be in no difficulty understanding what the parable is saying. Jesus tells us what he's getting at from the start. He has in mind those who hold a high opinion of themselves and who look down on others. That person exalts himself, says Jesus. What he is really saying to God is this: 'You don't need to change me, you know.'

By taking that view of himself, he builds a barrier against God, and therefore against the radical change of nature we need to enter the kingdom of heaven.

Somehow or other, we all indulge in this tendency to compare ourselves downward.

Despite feelings of insecurity or inferiority that may lurk within us, don't we secretly flatter ourselves that we are much better than some, and that, therefore, we have something to recommend us to the favour of God. After all, I'm not as bad as him, not as bad as that, we think; surely, in comparison with her, I've got much going for me. They need changing…but me? Why, every ordinary husband and wife gets expert at thinking of each other like that.

Jesus has a startling way of upsetting our comfortable view of ourselves. In the parable he rejects the man who looks down on others from his own high standards, and accepts the man whose life, up to that moment, had been a mess.

Why?

If you believe that what Jesus sees, God sees, what Jesus says to us, God is saying to us, you are faced here with a mighty big problem. Doesn't God value the qualities this Pharisee claims to stand for? Let me reinforce what is said about this man.

At least he went to a place of worship. More than that, he prayed to God.

And we believe him when he says he was not a robber, an evildoer, an adulterer. He was trying to live a decent life. Is it not an immense relief that there are men who are not financial sharks, who do honour their marriage vows? Let's have more of them.

He also stood for self discipline. He fasted twice a week, he tells us, cutting down on wasteful consumer expenditure, cutting out the luxuries. Can you imagine many modern guys cutting out the luxuries when they have a chance of living it up on expense accounts?

But there's something more commendable still about this man. He was prepared to sacrifice and cut down on his own standard of living to give one tenth of his income to support what we would now call third world needs. Rather than asking for a ten percent rise, he gave ten percent.

Can you see the kind of case you could build up for this man? Why, oh why, then, does God reject him? I mean, he's a pretty solid sort of chap like you and me. What is Jesus telling us?

Ultimately, it comes down to this—the man's attitude says loud and clear: 'God you don't need to change me.' He is, as Jesus puts it, exalting himself. He thinks he can stand before God and tell him his good points. He thinks he has the right to be accepted.

That shows the fatal flaw in him. We all share it. His standard of judging is all wrong. He measures himself by looking down at other people. Remember how he put it:

'God, thank you that I am not like other men.' When he tries to think of what God thinks of him, he chooses the man at the foot of the moral ladder, rungs below him, as his standard of comparison. We can always be falsely confident of our own righteousness if we look down at those round about us, rather than up to God's standards.

How do we do it? There are no end of ways. I guarantee you've run down other people's lifestyle, the way others bring up their children, the way people dress, or the circle they move in. Why is it that when you're with your special buddies, you take pleasure in being horrified at what 'he' does or 'she' does—the ones outside your circle.

Why do we do it? Doesn't it establish your superiority? Isn't that what we want confirmed? Ironically, of course, other people do the same about us. They see things to look down at in us. Nobody has a monopoly of looking down upon others. Jesus exposes this exclusive club mentality in us. We all take up our pinnacle positions. It merely serves to highlight what Jesus is telling us. While we get satisfaction from thinking we are better, we remain at the point where human nature—your nature, my nature—gets stuck and resistant to change.

Just like that Pharisee. He went home from church for the umpteenth time unchanged in his relationship to God. Self satisfied about how God and he were getting on. But still on the road that leads to destruction and showing few signs he even suspected he was in danger.

So we come to the second man. 'I tell you that this man', says Jesus, 'rather than the first man, went home accepted before God. For everyone who exalts himself will be humbled, and he who humbles himself will be exalted.'

I suspect this man had slipped embarrassed into church for the first time in years. He tried to hide himself away in the back seat. But Jesus tells us he went home that day, walking on air, elated that God had welcomed him, of all people. Yes! Why him, we ask, and not the apparently good guy?

God is not perverse. He treats men equally and does not prefer this second sort, who was probably as much of a rotter as the first man was respectable. As you know, the tax collectors of those days came near to being traitors to their own people. They were certainly collaborators with the occupying power, and we've seen often on television what people thought of collaborators during the last war. He would have been a hated, hardhearted type. And from what we know of similar characters like Zacchaeus, indeed he may well have been Zacchaeus, he would certainly have been a financial trickster, extorting money unjustly for his own benefit. Just the opposite to the Pharisee in that.

Why on earth then, does God accept him? I would ask you to see it like this. The Pharisee went into the church full of himself, went through the act of worship, and left the building no different from how he went in—proud, self congratulatory, and aware of his own superiority—untouched by God and not hearing what God had to say to him. The other man also went into church unaccepted by God, just as unacceptable as the Pharisee.

He would have remained so, except for one thing. Like the Pharisee, he also prayed, but his prayer was radically different. It shows he had realized he needed to be changed.

Something happened to make him see himself as he was and call upon God for acceptance like this.

He left a different man, a changed man, a man who had had real personal dealings with God. We need not go into church to pray that prayer. We can pray where we are and with the same results.

Let me leave you to think about our biological parable. Supposing frog had convinced tadpole that there was another kingdom he could enter. How could he get there? By being a very religious kind of tadpole, better by far than other tadpoles around him? It would have made no difference. A Pharisee tadpole is no more able live on dry land than a rotter of a tadpole. The crucial thing for both is that they experience the necessary change.

15

...But God Can

If human nature is to be changed for the better, a deep barrier to change must be removed in us. To show us that, Jesus told the story of the Pharisee and the tax collector.

The Pharisee had all the barriers up. He thought he was good enough as he was. Because he always looked down on others, he assumed he was OK. But his standard of judgement was all wrong. It never struck him he needed to be changed in his estimate of himself, others, and God. It was with that sort of attitude he prayed.

Jesus said God rejected him.

The other man, a tax collector, a notorious character, also prayed. That man, Jesus said, God accepted.

Why? How does it apply to you and me?

Let's call the tax collector in the parable Zacchaeus. The story of Zacchaeus is a follow up of that prayer, so it could well have been Zacchaeus who Jesus watched go into the temple to pray. What occurs later, in his home, is a thrilling example of what happens when God changes human nature.

Probably, Jesus spotted Zacchaeus caught in two minds about whether to go into church at all. Up and down the street he went before he plucked up enough courage to go in. Jesus tells us that when eventually he got in, he wanted to stay unnoticed. The Pharisee spotted him, of course, and turned away to avoid him. Zacchaeus sensed the rejection, and tried to avoid people's eyes. He certainly didn't feel he could look God in the face. 'He could not even look up to heaven,' says Jesus, noticing how distressed he was.

But, unlike the Pharisee, Zacchaeus prayed a life changing prayer: 'God, have mercy upon me, a sinner.'

First, let's be sure we understand what he did not mean when he prayed those words. There is a false prayer for mercy, just as there is a false prayer of self righteousness. We can pray for mercy in a way that amounts to a prayer of self-defence.

Supposing he had met the Pharisee's dismissive eye, and thought, quite rightly, 'Who does he think he is? He's not perfect either. Why doesn't he admit to a thing or two?' Supposing he then decided to pray like this.

'God, I thank you that I recognize my faults, not like some people I know. I may not be all that straight with money, I've fiddled an account or two, I've got the better of some unsuspecting clients, and my wife may not know of that brief affair, but who hasn't got blots. At least I'm admitting them.'

Lots of people are prepared to think in that vein and admit they are one of many who aren't all that perfect. But that becomes a defence of ourselves.

We are no worse than others, so we can't be as bad as all that. Instead of thinking we are better than others, we console ourselves with the thought they are no better than us. So we, too, end up comparing ourselves by the wrong standard—other people—and fail to take sin seriously. This leads us to take God's mercy for granted and we never come to God for forgiveness and new life.

That is not the way Zacchaeus prayed. What he longed for more than anything was that God would listen to his urgent cry for help, come, clean him up, and give him a new start.

'God, be merciful to me, a sinner.'

For the first time in his life Zacchaeus is alone with God. When a man truly turns to God with a burdened conscience like this, he doesn't think of other people at all. He looked down, not at other people, but down into his own heart, and he measured himself upward: 'God' and 'me'.

God himself was his standard of judgement. There are no other comparisons to make. Just two of them were involved. God and the sinner that he saw himself to be. He is terribly aware of how far off he is. But Jesus tells us that at that critical moment he did exactly what he needed to do. He made his urgent, personal call upon the mercy of God. And God accepted him.

It is at such a time of crisis in the human heart that God is nearest—a broken and a contrite spirit God does not despise. For he who humbles himself before God, shall be uplifted into the presence of God, says Jesus. When a man deals with God in this way, a change results in his life.

If you had a hidden camera outside the building when he went in and when he came out, you'd have seen the difference in his face and in every step he took. When this tax collector later meets Jesus, his prayer is answered.

He met him in a crowded street in Jericho. The crowd who turned out whenever Jesus came along didn't like seeing Zacchaeus around. He was a bad egg in their eyes. He wore the unacceptable face of capitalism, he had the dark side of financial scandal about him.

But the Bible tells us something the crowd doesn't know: Zacchaeus was determined to see Jesus. I hope you understand why. I hope you can identify. Any man who has faced his sin and cried out for the mercy of God wants to see who Jesus is. Why? Because Jesus is the mercy of God come to save us. One of the most famous verses in the Bible comes from this chapter—'The Son of Man came to seek and to save what was lost.'

Mind you, it may not be easy to get to Jesus in the kind of company you are in. Zac got no mercy from the crowd. 'Get lost' was their message to him as he tried to push through to the front to make up for his lack of inches. But he does not let other people or his own limitations prevent him getting to Jesus. Neither should we. Half hidden up a tree, he gets the most wonderful shock of his life. Jesus stops right there, and calls him by name:

'Zacchaeus, come down.'

Of course, Jesus meant 'Climb down from that tree.' But isn't there something apt about those words in a spiritual way?

Climbing down was exactly what the Pharisee refused to do. He was always looking down. No coming down, no humbling before God for him.

But when Zacchaeus had prayed that prayer he had already climbed down, inside himself. There was no barrier of pride or superiority in him, and no barrier of excusing himself either. He had humbled himself to call upon the mercy of God.

And here is the Son of God calling him down to him, in order to lift him up, a different man.

See how he does it: 'I want to come to your home and have a word with you.'

Nobody in that crowd approved of Jesus going to Zac's house. He was their political enemy, a social undesirable. You wouldn't see them calling on him.

But notice, Jesus did not see Zacchaeus primarily as a political or a social problem, though he was that. Here was a human being, conscious of how far he was from God, lost but seeking, in need of salvation. In other words, he was a person longing for a change of heart and to be right with God.

So Zacchaeus came down immediately and welcomed Jesus gladly. A spiritual revolution is going on in him. And it has radical effects on his whole disposition towards other people. His responsibilities, his duties to society are transformed.

But it cost him something.

First of all, he must have had a problem about Jesus coming to his home. The place was littered with things got from his ill-gotten gains. His office no doubt had evidence of the way he had swindled. 'Why, he can't come to my house,' was perhaps his first gut reaction.

Perhaps you think like that.

'You have no idea what goes on in our house,' you say. 'Nobody would ever believe it, but I'd be ashamed for him to come to my house. He might catch us at our worst.'

Jesus is the last person to keep out for that reason. He knows anyway. The greater the problem, the greater the need, and the more reason for you to welcome the Saviour.

'He's gone to be the guest of a sinner' sneered the crowd.

But of course he had. That's why he came into the world, and isn't that what Zacchaeus has seen himself to be?

'Today,' says Jesus to Zacchaeus, 'salvation has come to this house.' What a change came over that man and into that home. The evidence for it is plain to see.

This man, who had sought the mercy of God and had found Jesus, stood up among things that he had grabbed in greed and said, 'Lord, here and now I give half of all these things you see about me to the poor. And if I've cheated anybody, I give back four times the amount.'

Can human nature be changed? Let Jesus come in, and see what happens.

When Zacchaeus found Christ he found a new self and that new self began to express itself, as self always will. I bet that crowd began to cheer when he started writing cheques— 'Good old Zacchaeus'. Well, 'Good new Zacchaeus' would be more accurate. This restoration, reconciliation, this thinking of others shows that when a man changes his relationship to God through Christ, he begins to learn a new way of relationships to others, for Christ's sake.

This story is its own witness to how the vices of greed and merciless injustice begin to be solved when the hearts of men and women are changed.

Would we need so many conferences on the gap between the richer and poorer countries if every man who had ruthlessly feathered his own nest began to say, 'God, have mercy upon me, a sinner'? And if, when salvation came, he moved on to say, 'Lord, I restore it, and more, for your sake.'

Moral transformation is the supreme test of salvation even on the small scale of our lives. A few weeks after the Welsh Revival of 1904 began, a provision merchant received this letter from a parent: 'I have pleasure in sending you the enclosed Postal Order for two shillings. A child of mine received a two shilling piece instead of a penny as change in your shop eighteen months ago. I am returning it at the child's request. I trust it has not caused you to lose confidence in any of your employees.'

Restoring Our Life

16

The Birth and Life of Jesus

The Birth of Jesus Foretold and Fulfilled

> In those days Caesar Augustus issued a decree that
> a census should be taken of the entire world. So Joseph
> went up from Nazareth to Bethlehem to register with
> Mary.
>
> Luke 2: 1

Governments are always looking for new ways of taxation.
It was one of the reasons why the birthplace of Jesus was at
Bethlehem, believe it or not. It helps us realize how he was
born bang in the middle of everyday history.

Caesar Augustus, the heir of Julius Caesar, wanted to
collect more taxes, probably to finance his magnificent
rebuilding programme in Rome. And so, as Luke tells us, he
began to organize a poll tax. Augustus had a great love of
'admin'—details of census returns in his own handwriting
still exist.

Luke wants us to know about this particular census
because it affected a young carpenter called Joseph. It
required him to travel, with his wife Mary, from Nazareth
to Bethlehem. And when he got there, he would probably
have registered the birth of a child as well. The census
forms required it—name, occupation, property, kindred.
The child's name was Jesus. And because of that birth at
Bethlehem, Caesar Augustus who dominated Rome at the

height of its splendour, has his reign divided into BC and AD. The King of kings had been born in the royal city of David.

At this point Roman and biblical history meet. And this is where you have to be honest in your response to the Christmas message. Luke is known to be a historian who is careful about details. He did not invent Augustus, Quirinius, or the imperial admin department — they are part of the real Roman world. But neither did he invent the miracle of Jesus' birth, the angels or the fulfilment of prophecy at Bethlehem. They are part of the real world too. Luke is not making up these extraordinary bits, as if they were film fantasy like ET's arrival in America, or the return of the Jedi.

Not at all! Luke's whole point is that stupendous miraculous events happened in the middle of everyday matters like tax affairs. For example, God prophesied centuries before that a Saviour — Immanuel — God with us — would be born of a virgin and born in Bethlehem. The fulfilment of those prophecies involved, on the one hand a message from a real angel, and on the other, the administrative decision of a Roman Caesar. Both are part of the truth Luke is reporting.

If we could put ourselves in Joseph's shoes we might see how prophecy, miracle, and a government decree worked together in God's programme. Joseph had been pledged in marriage to Mary when she turns up with the likely story that an angel had told her she had conceived a baby by the Holy Spirit. Joseph couldn't take it. He was considering breaking off their betrothal when he, too, got an angel's message: 'Joseph, don't be afraid to take Mary as your wife because what is conceived in her is from the Holy Spirit. She'll give birth to a son, and you shall give him the name Jesus because he will save his people from their sins.' It precisely confirmed her story.

What finally put his mind to rest was the angel's reminder that Isaiah had prophesied this virgin birth, as a special sign from God about Immanuel. So he settled down with Mary in Nazareth. Nazareth was a long way from Bethlehem. And they both knew that if the child they were expecting was the one they had been told he was going to be, he would be born in Bethlehem. The prophet Micah had said so plainly.

And then came that official notice—today it would be a brown envelope through the door. The Roman authorities commanded everyone to go to their own town for the census. Joseph's home town was Bethlehem.

The tax office of a pagan empire cooperated unknowingly with a biblical prophecy and an angel's message. How clearly that must have reassured Joseph and Mary. It told them that their long journey, with Mary in her condition, over dusty desert tracks to Bethlehem was by appointment of the living God.

Now this is where the story begins to affect you and me. 'While they were there' Luke says, 'the time came for her to be delivered' You couldn't have blamed Joseph and Mary if they'd been hoping for some nice surprise in Bethlehem— some special arrangement for the birth at least. But the signs everywhere were the same—'NO VACANCIES'. Everyone was back in town.

So it had to be, as we all know, a manger.

What a disappointment! It could so easily have produced a crisis in the marriage. 'Why didn't you think and look ahead. Fancy leaving it all to the last minute. You've not given me much consideration.' Good job they had God's promise to trust. They could so easily have turned on one another. People are prone to turn on each other if they have a disappointing Christmas. Did you know that the queues for divorce build up after every Christmas holiday? People build their hopes on so much empty celebration, then turn on each other in disappointment. Empty bottles and lonely hearts become an epidemic.

The diminished threat of nuclear warfare fills us all with relief. But what about the actual, everyday warfare that flares up in the nuclear family, as sociologists call home these days. The post Christmas explosions in many a home blow neglected children out on to the streets.

Martin Luther once said 'When I see the wonder of a man and wife who are at one, I am so glad as if I were in a garden of roses.' Everyone would love to live in such a garden house.

I'm sure many will try hard and say, 'Let's be nice to each other this Christmas.' But even niceness is not enough. Doesn't every relationship start with people going out of their way to be nice to each other? Yet many end up in cold hatred. 'I'd never have thought it of them—they seem such nice people,' we say.

The fallacy as C. S. Lewis observes is this: we think nice people don't need to be saved. But they do. We all do. And the Christmas message is, above all, about salvation and the coming of the Saviour. Through him we can turn to God for forgiveness. And we can learn to stop turning on each other and turning away from each other. Instead of blowing apart, the family—mum and dad, boys and girls—becomes a power for good in the land.

Our disappointments at our failure to live loving, faithful lives are all part of the big problem of sin. What has the manger's message to offer us here? It goes right to the root of that big problem. In fact, what looked like a disappointment for Mary that night was actually one more part of God's careful plan to save us from our sin and set our lives right with God and right with each other. The manger points us straight to the cross—the place where Jesus died for sin and puts us right with God.

How, you ask, does the manger point that way?

Think back a minute. The Old Testament made it plain people could only come to God for forgiveness of sin by bringing a flawless lamb of sacrifice. As they did so, they were to believe that sacrifice was pointing forward to a perfect person who would one day come and take the penalty of their sins upon himself.

That night, in that Bethlehem manger, that perfect person came.

A manger may not seem an appropriate place for the Son of God to be born. But it is the perfect place for a lamb to be born, says Francis Schaeffer. And Jesus, the Son of God, is the Lamb of God who came to take away the sins of the world.

Two carols bring that out clearly:

> See, in yonder manger low
> Born for us on earth below,
> See the Lamb of God appears
> Promised from eternal years.

The second, by Christina Rossetti puts it like this:

> Child in a manger,
> Infant of Mary
> Outcast and stranger
> Lord of all.
> Child who inherits
> All our transgressions
> All our demerits
> On him fall.

Yes. All those transgressions that lie behind the disappointments—what shall we do about those transgressions? How can you prevent those wrong deeds and those damaging reactions from knocking your partner and you down into disappointment once again…despite all the gifts galore?

How can the high hopes of Christmas be fulfilled? There's only one way. We must receive God's Christmas gift of forgiveness and salvation. Glad tidings of great joy come when you receive the Saviour.

> He comes the broken heart to bind,
> the bleeding soul to cure
> and with the riches of His grace
> to enrich the humble poor.

The evidence that Christ is God's gift to us is all there in the prophecy, the miracles and the history surrounding the birth. That gift of God which is eternal life in Jesus Christ alone meets our deepest needs It's exactly what we need. Those who trust in him shall not be disappointed.

Some gifts can be disappointing. I know a young lad who woke up on Christmas morning, eagerly felt the wrappings around his presents and decided the hard and heavy one was the best. So he kept it till last. But, oh dear, when he opened it he found it was a metal music stand and he didn't like practising his music one bit. What a disappointment. He couldn't say, 'Thank you,' with any enthusiasm.

But what about when you unwrapped that gift and you were able to say 'It's just what I needed.' How the thanks flowed. Have you ever watched the face of someone who opens what they think will be an ordinary present and it turns out to be the greatest gift they have ever had? God's gift is far greater even than that. It is what you need, not merely at Christmas time, but for lifetime and eternity. He will not disappoint. Countless men and women have echoed each other in singing 'Thank you God for sending Jesus, Thank you Jesus that you came.'

One Christmas, a friend whose lifestyle and morals had been those of the soft drug culture said, 'Up till now I've been living every Christmas on the wrappings round the gift. Now I've found the gift of God in Jesus Christ.' Don't spend another Christmas missing the gift by playing with the wrappings of the season, whatever they are for you. Get beyond those wrappings to the gift of God. That gift can change your heart, your home, your marriage and your eternal destiny.

God's Gift Isn't Just for Christmas—It's for Life!

Most children enjoy a lie in during holidays, but it's not like that when Christmas Day comes round. Their light goes on when it's still dark—as dark as the Bethlehem hills where shepherds kept watch for prowlers. A light went on then, too, the glory of the Lord shining around them—a close encounter of the most brilliant kind.

A carol I heard at a school carol service, sung by two angelic little toughs, suggests one of those shepherds, called Philip, is a sceptic. He's off duty and asleep. His friend, enthralled by the glory of the Lord, tries to wake him. But Philip's not the kind who easily sees the light:

> Philip, awake I pray. Why waken me?
> Listen to what I say. O, let me be.
> See darkness is turned to light. How can that be?

Christmas comes at two levels. On one of them, there are definitely no sceptics, for whoever heard a child say on Christmas morning—' Why waken me? Let me be!' A close encounter with the rustle of wrapping paper and it's 'Quick, put the light on.' On Christmas Day of all days, on goes the light to see what they've been given. The child knows that the dark stops him seeing that gift.

Christmas is about another gift too, which our inner darkness prevents us seeing. God's surprise Christmas delivery, that tiny bundle named Jesus, born among the dark streets, is also the Light of Life come to take away our darkness. The Saviour come to bear away our sin upon the cross. The gift of God that offers us eternal life. Here sceptical hearts falter. How can that be? But unless we look for light, we remain in the dark about this gift of God. And staying in the dark about eternal life leaves a dark shadow in this life too.

The dark tragedy of loveless religion, the dark despair of an Iraq and a Somalia, the dark savagery of violence and vice, the dark rage of family feuding, the dark confusions of our own inner thoughts. When light does seem to dawn it's so intermittent; someone, somewhere blows a fuse and we're plunged back into our own moral power failures.

Isaiah's world was like that. But he had good news. People living in the shadow of death would see a great light. In Galilee a child would be born and a son given to us. And so he came, the Son of God, Jesus our Lord and Saviour, the inextinguishable Everlasting Light, come to us from heaven to shine into our lives, guiding us to paths of peace.

Last week a former alcoholic told me how that peace of Christ stems his anxiety, taking away fear of the bottle at Christmas. 'It's as if a light had been turned on inside me,' said someone else, about his close encounter of the personal, life-changing kind with the living Christ. The joy of God's forgiveness can turn people like us into lights in a darkening world. That's more important than even the joy upon the face of the child as the light goes on at Christmas. The child's welfare could depend on it. For God's gift isn't just for Christmas. It's for life.

The Lowly Majesty of the Servant Jesus

Which do you find you are better at—arguing with people or serving them?

Jesus spent a long time training his disciples to be servants. Then one day he overheard them arguing. It sounded as if they had learned little, for what they were arguing about was which of them was the greatest, a kind of seminar of ministerial students overheard staking their claims to be the greatest orator.

How did Jesus, the Servant King, handle these king-pin servants of his? Most importantly, what was it about him that radically changed these status seekers, for later they became some of the greatest servants for good the world has seen?

Home and the world at work can be a different place when people stop arguing and start helping. Evidently, the argument between the disciples had broken out in the street. We find the incident in Mark 9: 33:

> They came to Capernaum. When he was in the house, Jesus asked them, 'What were you arguing about on the road?' But they kept quiet because on the way they had argued about who was the greatest. Once indoors, Jesus asked: What were you arguing about out there?

They were speechless with shame. After all he'd shown them about serving one another, they'd shown more interest in their own pride of place. Keener to tell others how to serve, presumably. Even worse, status seeking had, for a moment, made them forget who their own leader was. Argument about who was the greatest among them missed the point entirely.

Only a few days earlier some of the disciples had glimpsed the glory and deity of Jesus on the mountain of transfiguration.

His purity had sparkled like a million diamonds, just as fresh snow and blue sea sparkle when the sun comes out over a fjord.

They saw the glory of Jesus on that mountain, outshining even nature's spectacular sights. And God did not leave them to guess what it meant:

'This is my beloved Son,' said the voice from heaven.

They had had a breathtaking view of the surpassing glory of this Jesus, yet he had chosen the Servant's way to make servants out of self regarding sinners. His majesty was veiled in meekness, their destiny bound up in his sacrifice on the cross for their sakes. He had spoken about it, just before they started on their competing ego trips. Thus their shamed silence. A hymn tells us who he is:

> Thou art the everlasting Word
> The Father's only Son
> God, manifestly seen and heard
> And heaven's beloved One.

Lowly Majesty

Our question seems to have focused into this. Does our concept of status leave us indifferent to serving others? We value quality of service, of course, but who likes to be thought of as a servant? Jesus calls an emergency meeting of his leadership team to talk this through:

> Sitting down, Jesus called the Twelve and said, 'If anyone wants to be first, he must be the very last, and the servant of all.' He took a little child and had him stand among them. Taking him in his arms, he said to them, 'Whoever receives one of these little children in my name receives me; and whoever receives me does not receive me, but the one who sent me.'

Look, he says, I've given you the task of leading from the front in Christian work, but the only way is to be willing to serve in the lowliest place. He takes a child to enforce his point. Children were far from pampered in the ancient world. Just the opposite; neglect abounded. So, when Jesus takes a little child in his arms he is deliberately calling attention to those who were regarded as insignificant. He is showing that a mark of real greatness is to serve those who aren't noticed.

It's one thing to be paid well for providing quality of service, but what about being a servant to the helpless who have no way to repay you? I can't say I know much about that, but I know how lovely it was to hear from an orphan girl in Haiti, who ended her letter 'I love you! Pray for me!'

Of course Jesus is not only showing us how to serve. He is saying something about himself. In an amazing paradox, which it is easy to miss, he lets us into the secret of who he, the lowly servant, really is. The person who receives the lowly, the insignificant, in my name, receives me, Jesus says.

But now notice the paradox in the next phrase, to receive Jesus—the lowly Servant who gave himself for us—is to receive God in the highest: if you receive Jesus, you receive God who sent him. Jesus is telling us who he is as he demonstrates his lowliness. The jewel of his deity flashes in its earthenware casket. The one God sent to be the Saviour of the World is the lowly Jesus who bids us come. He is God—manifestly seen and heard among us. There lies the marvel of salvation.

Of course, we can argue about that. But I wonder if that just means we are better at arguing than serving? Will you take another look at the way he served and why he served? It overturns our self importance.

He who shares the glory of God, made himself of no reputation.

Let the glory that surpasses the sparkling fjord flash in your mind, and then...think of a desperate couple in a farmyard shed. The contrast comes out in this hymn:

> From heaven you came, helpless babe,
> Entered our world, Your glory veiled.
> Not to be served, but to serve,
> And give your life that we might live.
> This is our God, the Servant King,
> He calls us, now, to follow Him.

17

The Meaning of the Cross

The Plot

In this chapter we shall follow Jesus on his way to the cross. We pick up the story as a titanic battle approaches its climax. Jesus makes his final moves to defeat the powers of darkness. He does so through the cross.

Luke prepares us for the drama of what's ahead by exposing a plot. Judas is playing a double game. He'd secretly defected to the authorities who badly wanted to be rid of Jesus, but feared the reaction of ordinary people. When Judas turned up, offering to help in the arrest, it solved their problem. They needn't risk it in public. Judas volunteered to identify Jesus in the dark by a kiss of greeting. He agreed the price—thirty pieces of silver. They have stuck as chilling symbols of betrayal.

The plot to deliver Jesus to death is well known. But there are two plans here. Jesus has one too. He had come into the world for one overriding purpose—to die. So Judas's plot fits in to his purpose. As the cross looms, Jesus is ultimately in control. He wasn't going to let Judas 'get him' until he'd kept the Passover and instituted the Lord's Supper. By linking the two, he wanted to get through to his disciples the meaning of his death. It was not a disaster; it was a deliverance. As the Passover recalled how God had delivered Israel from captivity, so Jesus' death was to deliver us from our sins. Remembering that, on the eve of his own death, would imprint its meaning on the minds of his disciples for ever. Judas musn't interfere with that.

So Jesus held him off by taking steps to cover his tracks. He'd made an arrangement with a house owner in Jerusalem to reserve a room for them. Not even Peter and John knew that, because when he sent them into the city to prepare the Passover room they ask: 'But where? How will we find it?'

It seems as if Jesus had set up a previously agreed signal and password to enable them to do so: 'As you enter the city,' he says, 'watch for a man carrying a water jar.' That would identify the contact because invariably women carried the water jars. 'Follow him into a house and say to the owner, "The teacher asks, 'Where is the guest room where I may eat the Passover?'" He will show you a large upper room.' By the time Judas found out where that Passover room was, it would be too late to betray Jesus to the authorities.

So they all gathered in that upper room. As he poured out the wine Jesus reminded them that his blood is to be shed for the forgiveness of sins. It was Judas's last chance to turn aside from his part in the plot to kill. But the money was in his pocket. Bit by bit, avarice had hardened him. For some time he'd been lining his own pocket from money meant for the poor. Yet he'd protested that Mary's box of precious ointment had been wasted on Jesus: 'Why wasn't it sold and the money given to the poor?' By then he was capable of betraying even Jesus for a price. But as he went out into the night it is Jesus who is in control. The two plans, one of destruction the other of deliverance, interlock. Through the cross, Jesus took on man's real enemies — sin and death — and triumphed. That victory delivers us. The cross breaks their power.

Gethsemane

One night a man went out into a garden with his friends. Probably a full moon lit up the shadowy paths, an owl hooted, crickets made their special noises. They trod on sticks and brushed against branches.

'Stay here. I want to pray alone,' he said.

When we think of a garden we usually think of a place of peace, relaxation, refreshment, and meditation.

But the man in this garden is burdened with such overwhelming stress that he almost dies under it. He falls on his face in dismay as he considers the most agonizing prospect that has ever confronted anyone. Here in the quiet of the night, with his friends asleep around him, Jesus is on his own. He cries out to God with the question many of us only ask as a debating point. The question was this: Father, can't there be another way? Is this the only way to save people from the results of sin?

Jesus praying in the garden of Gethsemane is full of mystery which we cannot fathom. But it is full of meaning too. It helps us understand that the cross is God's way of saving the world. One of the biggest questions we can ever face is, why does Christianity claim to be the only way to God? We all have our views about God and the way to heaven. We are free to disagree and discuss, to live and let live. And so it should be, especially in our pluralist society. But why only one way? Could that be true?

Jesus' prayer in Gethsemane is perhaps the best way to approach that question. The way ahead for him was so terrible that he prayed this prayer with sweat like drops of blood pouring down his body, struck with horror, deeply stressed, in mental anguish. 'Father, if it's possible, is there any other way?'

The one who is the way, the truth, the life asked that question. He knew the answer, he had come into the world to save us. He had been telling his disciples that more and more. There was a 'must' about his death.

And yet as he faced it, the horror so appalled him that three times he asked if there was the possibility of there being any other way…'Yet thy will be done.' How do we understand this horror?

It certainly wasn't panic, or despair or fear of dying. Socrates faced death with great calm; Stephen with great joy. Jesus didn't lack these men's moral courage. Yet 'no man feared death like this man,' says Luther. Why? It wasn't physical death he feared like that. So many face that with faith. I've seen someone do so this week. Why then the horror in the reaction of Jesus?

The Bible's explanation lies in the unique reason for his death. The weight that bore down on his sinless soul was the weight of the world's sin. His perfect purity shrank from the prospect of bearing our iniquity and taking the judgement of God upon it. What he was about to do for us almost broke him before he died. Had there been any other way for our sins to be forgiven, Gethsemane would have been the moment to show it.

Arrest

To be suddenly arrested while you lie dozing in the dark is not a pretty thought. It's a police state technique, often done through an informer. It happened to the disciples in Gethsemane after Judas had betrayed their meeting place. Numbed by sleep, they were thrown into panic when a hostile arrest party disturbed them in the dark.

Judas moved to identify Jesus. But again Jesus shows who is in control of these events leading to his death. He steps forward: 'Are you betraying me with a kiss, Judas?' But for the disciples, it's a shattering crisis. It sinks in. This was a betrayal, an arrest. Peter, who fancied himself as bodyguard to Jesus, swings a sword without asking and slashed off the ear of the high priest's servant.

This surely was the flashpoint at which everything could have gone out of control and the disciples put to the sword. But into the hubbub comes the peaceful authority of Jesus. His restraining words convey both 'No more of this!' and 'Don't let things escalate!' It's not the disciples he's restraining but the soldiers, stopping them overreacting to Peter's impetuosity. As usual his authority knows no limits. He steps into the ruck, stopping a massacre—just by his word. And his disciples are saved.

Then comes another moment of moral power. Jesus had taught his disciples to love their enemies. As his enemies crowd in for the kill, he shows them what he means. The posse sent out to arrest him, watch a miracle of love from someone they were treating like a criminal: 'and he touched his ear and healed him.' Though Jesus' hands were healing hands, violent hands were now laid on him. When the disciples see this they flee, thinking it's all up. But Luke reminds us this is the point where Jesus deliberately surrenders: 'This is your hour—when darkness reigns,' he says. Two plans are afoot. Through the evil plan of destruction God is working his plan of salvation.

These men were agents of the evil powers of darkness; underhand, cowardly, snatching at their hour, being permitted by God to bring the Son of the Highest down into humiliation and death—not because he's not mighty enough to prevent it, but because he is mighty and merciful enough to deliver himself up for our salvation, that we might go free.

C. S. Lewis vividly describes this self surrender in the Chronicles of Narnia. He tells how Lucy and Susan watch as the great lion Aslan gives himself up to the Witch in order that Edmund, who has become her captive by siding with her, might go free. 'For a moment even the Witch seemed to be struck with fear when she saw the great lion pacing towards them...Lucy and Susan held their breaths, waiting for Aslan's roar and his spring upon his enemies. But it never came...'Bind Him' cried the Witch...[They] rushed in when they found he made no resistance at all. Between them they rolled the huge Lion over on his back and tied his paws together, cheering as if they had done something brave, though, had he chosen, one of those paws would have been the death of them all. Then, they began to drag him towards the Stone Table.'

Trial

British justice, once a model for the world, has taken some knocks recently. Roman justice was also famous for its fairness. But it has one huge blot. Jesus was condemned to death because Pilate was swayed by a first century rent-a-crowd chanting 'Crucify him'. Their voices 'prevailed, and Pilate gave sentence that what they asked for should be done.'

Pilate's sentence shows what happens when the legitimate power of the state comes under the influence of the mob. Even mighty Rome, the fount of just law, could not retain its integrity or preserve justice when it turned its back on Jesus and the truth.

'What is truth?' Pilate asked Jesus. He seemed to ask it, not as a genuine enquirer, but cynically: 'Truth! What is truth?— Nobody has the answer to that one.' It left him evasive, trying to pass the buck; heartless, too, keen to save his own position as Caesar's friend, even if it meant condemning an innocent man. In the end, he was clever enough to find a way of ditching responsibility. He washes his hands of the whole affair. So, when he gave the mob what it wanted, it wasn't truth that won but his own self interest.

Pilate holds up a mirror to our own day as we see the mob mentality threaten streets and classrooms. That mentality takes over whenever leaders are cynical about the truth. Pilate's interaction with Jesus exposes our failings as well as his. Whoever we are, facing Jesus and having to decide who he is, puts us all on the spot. Is it truth or the prevailing majority?

But Jesus didn't die merely because Pilate was a self regarding judge. There's more to it than that. Much deeper things are going on here. Because Pilate is called upon to judge the Son of God, he's caught up in a unique, awesome event. His sentence has titanic implications and he serves a higher purpose. Pilate becomes, all unwitting, a figure representing God, the eternal Judge.

How can that be? The two things of greatest significance Pilate did will show you how. First of all, Pilate pronounced Jesus to be faultless. Several times he said it. 'I find no fault in him.' He cleared him.

Yet, secondly, having made it perfectly clear no charge could be pinned on Jesus, he delivered him to death.

For different reasons, that is also what God did. God, too, affirmed the perfection of Jesus, his beloved Son. And God, too, delivered Jesus up to the cross.

Father and Son cooperate, the judge and the innocent volunteer do something together, for us, at infinite cost, in perfect love and justice. Jesus identifies with us without limit. He takes our sins, guilt, death, judgement—the lot. We are acquitted and go free, for God the just and merciful judge drops the charges against us.

Barabbas

There was a man in Jerusalem who couldn't believe his luck. He was a first century political terrorist—the type who would plant a bomb in a crowded street. He was interned along with two others and due to be executed for murder.

But he was set free—by popular vote. When the imperialist police released him, I can imagine what they said. 'Hey! You! Your luck's in! Pilate has bowed to the crowds. They voted you out of here. Instead they've condemned that man some claim is King of the Jews. If you're quick, you'll see him die—in your place.'

Barabbas, for he's the one we're talking about, must have thought it rich to be set free in exchange for a king. In a later age, it would have got the world's press and television cameras jostling at the prison gates as he came out.

Who knows? Perhaps Barabbas did join the crowds and watch three figures stagger up a hill with their crosses—two of them his former cell mates. The other, the third man, in the place where he should have been, was Jesus.

The Bible constantly makes universal principles out of individual incidents in the life of Jesus. Because one went to his death, another man lived. The exchange meant death for Jesus, life for Barabbas. The New Testament is full of that liberating timeless truth. Jesus dies in our place, so we— anyone, anywhere—can be set free from condemnation. That is good news. But how is it possible?

That becomes clearer if we watch those three men going up the hill to Calvary. Again the Bible presents those individuals in a representative way. On the central cross is Jesus who dies for the sins of the world. And there is a man on his right, another on his left. They too are dying. But the contrast in their attitude to Jesus is total. One criminal taunted Jesus and hurled insults at him. He represents the unrepentant. He's deeply bitter. Could any man on a cross be anything but bitter?

Yet the miracle is this. The other criminal turns to Jesus. The change in his attitude is startling. He rebukes his comrade. 'Don't you fear God since you too are dying? We are punished justly, for we're getting what we deserve. But this man has done nothing wrong.'

This is a terrorist moved to a change of heart through the suffering of Jesus upon the cross. He calls out in faith: 'Jesus, remember me when you come into your kingdom.' The only possibility for this man is faith in the Saviour. He can do nothing now but show radical repentance. And Jesus receives him. That man is there to remind us that none, however far gone, is beyond the range of God's forgiveness.

I've never forgotten a former IRA terrorist in Northern Ireland deeply convince a conference of young people, beyond any shadow of a doubt, that Jesus had replaced his bitter hate with love when he had turned to him in repentance and faith.

18

The Resurrection of Jesus

He Is Risen

'Why do you look for the living among the dead? He is not here. He is risen.'

What we call our mind's eye is a very powerful thing. If you have a splendid garden bursting out in all the flowers and colours of spring, you are able to picture it all in your mind's eye now. What if, later today, asks Francis Schaeffer, you watch a crowd of vandals throw rubbish from dustbins, ashes, coal dust, rubble, tins, plastic all over it, until everything that gave you such joy is ruined. What happens to the picture in your minds eye? It too is destroyed. Another takes its place.

If you have seen gruesome things in battle or in accidents, the pictures that remain in your mind's eye can sometimes blot out everything else. 'I keep on seeing it,' we say, 'I can't get it out of my mind.'

The disciples who went to the tomb of Jesus early that morning had seen and heard those cruel nails hammered in. At least some had watched as his physical frame had gone horribly out of joint as he hung there for hours. Their mind's eye was still full of those brutal facts. The true picture they had of Jesus as God's Son, alive with love and truth, that picture had been obliterated, blow by blow, and replaced by another awful picture—the picture of his sufferings and death. It left them in black grief and despair.

Yet, these same people were soon to be gloriously transformed. What could possibly have removed the darkness of those crushing facts? Don't forget they needed the evidence for the resurrection even more than we do, because they had seen him die. And their mind's eye was full of the force of those facts. His death had been no hallucination—they hadn't been 'seeing things', as we say, at Calvary. So his resurrection would have to be real too. 'Seeing things' that were not real—visions or hallucinations— would never have obliterated the impact of his death. Only other facts, stronger and more compelling than the death of Jesus, could convince them Jesus had conquered death.

And that is exactly what began to happen to them. Bit by bit, their minds were presented with evidence so convincing that this bereaved group of people became elated with joy. Jesus was risen from the dead.

The facts mount up. First, the huge stone blocking the entrance to the tomb, sealed and guarded for security, was rolled aside.

Secondly, they could not find the body. They looked and looked in that small tomb. 'But this is impossible!' Yet the tomb was empty except for the grave clothes lying there, and Jesus—gone.

Thirdly, their minds, hammered and wearied by death's affairs, received a heavenly stimulus. Two angels in dazzling apparel stood among them. It was a sensation. And deep in those saddened lives something mightier than death began to restore them. Extraordinary facts of life began to stamp out the picture of death.

Fourthly, they were asked a question. And what a question. 'Why do you look for the living among the dead?' They were really being told, 'You need not have come to the tomb at all on the third day, if you wanted to find Jesus. He is not here. He is risen. You don't come to a tomb to look for the resurrection and the life. Remember, remember, he told you that on the third day he would rise. Didn't he tell you he had come to give his life a ransom for many and he had the power to take up that life again after three days?'

These are some of the things that now came back to them. And these new facts they were experiencing all began to reverse the despair they had collapsed into. The numbness of grief that so many of you will know all about began to roll away like that stone before the tomb. The cruel shock barrier of the past few days is broken through.

It isn't just the memory of what Jesus said that was being restored to them. Jesus himself came—to one of them, to two together, to seven at the lakeside, to ten, to eleven, to five hundred—at different times and places over forty days. 'Jesus came, and stood among them and said "Peace be with you."'

I find almost a smile of divine humour here. They had gone looking for him among the dead and were too late. They had missed him because he was alive. Now he comes to them. Have you been looking for me? Peace…

Maybe you are looking for something—meaning, answers, hope and yet you feel you are being asked to believe the unbelievable. If so, don't just puzzle over the resurrection. Concentrate first on Jesus himself. Of course the resurrection would be unbelievable if we were claiming it for any other historical figure, whoever he be. There is tremendous presumption against resurrection in every such case. It would be unbelievable.

But in the case of Jesus, the presumption—that is, the grounds for accepting it—is all the other way. The world has only seen one Jesus. In his case alone the resurrection fits: it fits into the person he was, his moral perfection, his miraculous power, and his unique claims.

The Gateway Home

One Saturday morning, between Good Friday and Easter Day, I was preparing a message on the resurrection of Jesus. Glancing out of my study window, I saw a gaily decorated bridal car in front of an undertaker's house that had 'Funeral Home' written boldly alongside its door. A moment later, through the door there stepped a bride alight with white.

For a moment I stared unbelievingly because it seemed so out of place where mourners usually gather—until I saw the parable of Easter Day. At the spot where we expect to find weeping, there was joy; someone was stepping out towards the first day of a new life.

When Mary and the others went to the tomb that morning, they expected nothing but death. It was a place of death. But they found the reverse. 'And behold, an angel of the Lord rolled back the stone. His appearance was like lightning and his raiment white as snow.' Out of the door of a grave came an angelic messenger of life and loveliness. 'He is not here. He is risen.' It was the opposite of what was expected. Indeed, resurrection is so opposite to everyone's experience it is possible for the whole tremendous event to pass us by, because we fail to take it in.

Death comes within our experience. It is something we all know about. And, because on Good Friday we watch someone die, there are many who feel the drama of the cross in a very similar way to feeling a great Shakespearean tragedy. That completely misses the meaning. It is no tragedy. We speak of triumph. But we can only feel and know it to be so when we see that the resurrection is not just a triumph for Jesus, but for me. The last thing we feel when watching a Shakespearean tragedy is that here is a triumph for me. Remember Macbeth's reaction to his wife's death. After all his striving ambitions, his conclusion about life is that it is a meaningless series of days strung one after another, ending in nothing. All our yesterdays and tomorrows lead to a 'dusty death'. Life is like 'a brief candle...a walking shadow...a tale told by an idiot, full of sound and fury signifying nothing.'

Is death so omnipotent? Must it cast its black shadow over life so completely that you have to agree with that? Or with those students who raised a banner asking, 'Is there life before death?' let alone after.

No! Enough of that! Death has no answers, so let us look to Jesus who brought about the death of death. His triumph can be yours and mine too. To know how, let's speak of some of the simple pictures the Bible uses to link his resurrection to our death.

Firstly, if he is your saviour, his resurrection makes your death as harmless as a shadow. 'Yea, though I walk through the valley of the shadow of death, I will fear no evil, for thou art with me.' There are many who fear walking through dark shadows, because evil may lurk there. 'Men fear death like children fear the dark.' We have all heard children say 'Come with me,' when they are afraid of the dark. Shadows aren't frightening when there is someone strong with you who can deal with any evil there. We all have to go through the valley of the shadow of death, and, if left to ourselves to 'go it alone', none of us looks forward to going through it. But the person who trusts in the risen Christ knows two things that can make all the difference.

It makes a difference because our Lord Jesus went through death for us, to deal with the evil in the shadow. There was darkness for three hours at Calvary when he endured the wrath of God upon sin. He went through that for us.

It makes a difference because our Lord Jesus also went through death in another sense—in the sense that he came out the other side. He rose again. He did not stay dead, there in the valley of the shadow. And neither does the believer. 'Because I live you shall live also.' We go through into the presence of Christ, and 'heaven's morning breaks and earth's vain shadows flee.'

The resurrection of Jesus takes the sting out of death. As some fear shadows, so others are afraid of stings. One summer I watched a wasp fly in through the window of my study and then disappear in the shadow cast by the curtain. The ominous link of shadow and sting. But no-one fears a sting that is withdrawn. The Bible says the sting of death is sin. That is the poisonous, harmful element in death. Once removed, we can say, 'O death! Where is your sting?…Thanks be to God who gives us the victory through our Lord Jesus Christ.' The victory he gives is eternal life.

Did you hear the story of that eighteen month old child in Africa? He was going through the teething stage. His parents saw him out on the lawn with a poisonous snake in his mouth. They ran out, terrified, only to discover he had bitten off the snake's head!

Christ was once described as 'that dangerous child.' He was born that man no more may die and he achieved that for his people by wreaking harm and havoc on the power of death. He bruised the head of Satan, that old serpent who held humankind in fear of death, and he withdrew the sting.

The resurrection of Jesus turns our death into sleep. Here we see the effect of his resurrection softening our grief. Paul the apostle says: 'I do not want you to be ignorant about those who sleep, or grieve like those who have no hope. For we believe that Jesus died and rose again to obtain salvation for us, so that whether we are awake or have fallen asleep (died) we might live with him' (1 Thess. 4: 13; 5: 9–10). This picture of sleep is a touching one. When you put a child to sleep you say, 'See you in the morning.' A believer in the risen Saviour who lays a fellow believer to rest says, 'See you in the morning.' Are you afraid of that sleep? Not if, when you wake, you will be with Christ.

So his resurrection means the separation of death is not final. It leads the believer home. Separation is an absence, a void, a yearning. But the Word of God says neither life nor death can separate us from the love of God in Christ Jesus the Lord. Nothing, not even the separation of death separates permanently. Part of the triumph of Jesus being our triumph is that separations are different when there are glad reunions ahead. That is not sentiment but the sheer victory of a risen saviour who tells us that if we trust him, death is finally the gateway home.

He is the only one who came from heaven and is as familiar with heaven as we are with home. Jesus says, 'I came forth and have come from God. He sent me. ' And that is why he can say, 'In my father's house [that is, in my home] are many mansions.' He has prepared a place for us, so his home can be our home too.

What a contrast Jesus' words of assurance present to the desperate uncertainty of the greatest human minds. Listen:

> Ah, but to die, and go we know not where!…
> The weariest and most loathed earthly life
> Is a paradise, to what we fear of death.

That is the sad picture of a world on the run from God. Something terrible has gone wrong in the relationship between man and God for those words to be uttered. What brought John Wesley to realize he was not right with God was the contrast between his fear of death in that mighty storm in the Atlantic and the calm assurance of the families of Moravian believers who were fellow passengers.

To be without God and without home, so that your last move—from time to eternity—will not be homeward, but to the everlasting prison house of an unpardoned soul. Is that not why people dread the move?

But there is no place like home. It is only when relationships break down and love is absent, that that is not true. I remember a woman screaming outside our house at 2am: 'Don't take me home—not home.' Things needed to be put right.

Jesus puts us right with God. He says there is a place in the Father's house, so your last call can be a glad home call. He alone ensures that. He opened the kingdom of God to all believers: believers, not achievers. 'Every man must do his own believing as every man must do his own dying,' said Luther. To refuse to believe on the Lord Jesus is to die alone.

But, says Jesus, 'Let not your heart be troubled. Believe in God. Believe also in me.' He is the way to God. A place is held for you. A permanent place, for the life Jesus gives us is eternal life.

And it depends entirely upon what he has done. 'The gift of God is eternal life through Jesus Christ our Lord.' The difference between any man-made religion and the gospel of our Lord and Saviour Jesus Christ lies here. Religion says you must try and achieve. Religion is essentially something you try and do. The Christian gospel is about what has been done for you. Christ has achieved, we must believe. And believe in him we must. No one else has lived a perfect life but he; no one else has died for the sins of the whole world but he. None but he can take the sting from death, the evil from the shadow, and remove what separates us from God.

It is Jesus who opens the kingdom of heaven to all who believe. So trust him, and he will not keep you out.

> I know that my Redeemer lives:
> What joy the blest assurance gives!
> He lives to raise me from the grave
> And me eternally to save.
>
> He lives my mansion to prepare
> And he will bring me safely there.
> He lives, all glory to his name!
> Jesus unchangeably the same!

Come to your Right Mind

'If the dead are not raised, let us eat and drink, for tomorrow we die. Do not be deceived, bad company ruins good morals. Come to your right mind and sin no more: for some have no knowledge of God' (1 Cor. 15: 32–4).

'If the dead are not raised...' It is not at all unusual for people to deny the resurrection. We might say, 'Well, what of it? Let's just get on with living now.' But it is a strange thing that if we deny the resurrection, it not only makes dying a sad business, but it can often make living a sad and bad business too.

H. G. Wells used to say the disciples made up the resurrection of Jesus to give the whole story a happy ending. But have you noticed how people who say the resurrection is an invented happy ending often come themselves to an unhappy ending? In his later years, Wells said: 'In spite of my disposition to a brave looking optimism, I perceive that the universe is bored with man; it is turning a hard face to him. Homo sapiens is played out.' He wrote, too, of man's 'mind at the end of its tether'.

You may recall Bertrand Russell's famous words in *Why I Am not a Christian*: 'When I shall die I shall rot, and nothing of my ego will survive...There is darkness without and when I die, there will be darkness within. There is only triviality for a moment, and then nothing.' Toward the end of his life he wrote a gloomy book about the human race called *Has Man a Future?*

But, like you and me, the ordinary person usually covers up that despair in the face of life's emptiness. Do you face up to the implications for life, if it is true, that it all ends in nothing? I doubt it. What we tend to do is to work or entertain ourselves to death, or insure ourselves against death, rather than think about it. An insurance company once advertised with the question, 'If you had died yesterday, what would you be worth today?' It was urging us to make your death worthwhile for at least someone. But worthwhile for someone else, of course, not for you. Now it is caring and protective of us to think of death in terms of insurance for someone else. But God's care and protection includes you too: he assures us that if you die in Christ today, you will be worth all the glory that God offers you for all eternity. 'Today', said Jesus to the dying thief who repented, 'you shall be with me in paradise.'

When the Apostle Peter wrote to persecuted Christians in the Roman Empire, he told them that the resurrection of Jesus had given them a living hope and an inheritance that would never perish, spoil or fade—kept in heaven for them. You do not find much despair there, either in this life or for the life to come, do you? D. L. Moody once said, 'One day you'll read in the papers that D. L. Moody is dead. Don't believe it. I shall be more alive then than I have ever been.'

But if we do say the dead are not raised, if we think this life is the whole show and the curtain comes down never to rise again, we are only being despairingly honest to think that we are no more than animals with certain pleasurable but temporary desires to be indulged, so 'let us eat and drink, for tomorrow we die.'

If we think like that, then the quality of life, our moral standards of living, will decline and homes and families, the old, the teenager, the child and the unborn will suffer.

'Do not be deceived,' says 1 Corinthians 15: 32, 'bad company ruins good morals.' That is, if we keep company long enough with the lie that this life is all there is, you are keeping very bad company. That idea will affect not only your thinking, but it will drag down your moral living standards. Our age has been influenced by definitions of man ranging from 'man is lived sex' to 'man is what he eats.' So is it surprising that many seem to live for sex and live to eat? Men become the naked ape which some tell us we are.

Any average parent and teenager would agree at least on this—we are confused about, and have difficulty in agreeing about, what is right and wrong. The reason is we have been so long in the company of ideas that have ruined good morals. Those ideas are linked to a rejection of the resurrection of Jesus. Russell, whose words about death I quoted earlier, went on record as saying that the first of his Ten Commandments would be 'Thou shalt not be certain of anything'—by which he meant right and wrong.

George Bernard Shaw once dismissed the resurrection like this: 'The ultimate statistic is that one out of one dies.' Listen to the kind of moral advice stemming from that. When a young woman asked Shaw for some moral guidelines, he replied, probably with a mischievous twinkle, 'Try how wicked you can be. It is precisely the same experiment as being as good as you can be.' In other words, if there is no God, anything goes: why not experiment?

What has this passage from God's Word to say to a generation as confused as ours? 'Come to your right mind'—to your senses—'and sin no more, for some have no knowledge of God.'

First it says, God is knowable. We can have a personal knowledge of God—indeed we must, if we are to know ourselves, and how to live. Have you read William Golding's *Lord of the Flies*? A group of ordinary schoolboys cast away on a desert island eventually tear themselves apart with violence. One of the lads cries out: 'What are we? Humans? Animals? Savages?' Well…who are we? If we do not come to know God, we cannot know. Not to know, results in purposelessness. Often that issues in lawlessness.

When the Mods and Rockers had their first pitched battle in Clacton in 1964, someone wrote in the press: 'We adults did not give these teenagers a firm purpose in life.' It is the decay of that purpose and meaning in life that has led to increasing social disturbance. If we do not know God, we have no meaning and we cannot convey one to others either. And do you know what we do to cover that up? We compensate by seeking power, which for the majority means more money, and for the minority, more violence; or we compensate for lack of meaning by reaching out for more pleasure—'let us eat and drink.'

'Do not be deceived…' continues the verse, 'and sin no more.' God is knowable and not to know him is sin. If bad company ruins good morals, God's company restores good morals. God has told us he is our Creator and Saviour. If we suppress that truth we are frustrated in our search for meaning. We are meant to know and live with a holy God for ever. Without him, we are left without a real reason for living.

Well, how do we find that purpose? 'Come to your right mind,' says our passage. What does it mean to be in our right mind? It means we are to come to know the God who raises the dead. And how does that happen? Believe in the everlasting God who not only sent his Son to die for us, but raised him from the dead.

The ultimate statistic is, therefore, not 'one out of one dies.' Full stop. Not at all. 'The love of Christ constrains us... one died for all, that they who live might no longer live for themselves, but to him who for their sakes died and rose again' (2 Cor. 5: 14–15). Yes, Jesus died. But that was not just one more statistic on the burial register of Jerusalem. Jesus and the resurrection was the overwhelming message of the early church.

The consequences of denying the resurrection are all about us. Are you just living to yourself, doing your own thing, inventing your own morality irrespective of what God says, or of whether you or someone else gets hurt? Jesus died for your sake and rose again, so that you might know God and therefore live for him, for each other, and for ever. Jesus fills our lives with his love and empties our graves by his power.

God calls us to take account of his power over death. It is easy to scorn when you have not come to your right mind. Do you remember the story of Jairus' daughter in the New Testament? She had died, and all the mourners had gathered around. Jesus called in and he said, 'She is not dead; she is asleep.' And we read: 'they laughed him to scorn, knowing that she was dead.' We sympathize with them. Their knowledge was correct as far as it went. She was dead; and they were understandably scornful. But they did not know the power of God. And Jesus said, 'Little girl I say to you, arise.'

Has the pressure of this world's thinking made you leave out of account God's power over death? Many think of death as 'that undiscovered country, from whose bourn no traveller returns,' so how can anyone know? The Easter message says, not true—one Traveller has returned to bring us glad tidings. Jesus said: 'I am he that liveth and was dead, and behold I am alive for evermore.'

As you travel on, destiny unknown, are you perplexed like that man in the poem?

> 'Is there anybody there?' said the traveller,
> Knocking on the moonlit door...
> And he knocked upon the door a second time
> 'Is there anybody there?' he said....
> But no-one descended to the traveller
> Where he stood perplexed and still.

Again, not true. We need not be perplexed. Jesus has descended:

> He came down to earth from heaven
> Who is God and Lord of all.

There is an answer to the question, 'Is there anybody there?' The God who is there came here, into this world to bring us there—into his presence. Seek him and you shall find. You shall come to your right mind. Do not go aimlessly through life, like a rich tramp, picking up the scraps of life, all dressed up to eat, drink and be merry, but with no home finally to go to.

> No more we doubt thee, glorious Prince of life;
> Life is nought without thee; aid us in our strife;
> Make us more than conquerors through thy deathless love;
> Bring us safe through Jordan to Thy home above.

19

The Ascension of Jesus

Our Final Move

Most of us find moving house stressful. Some dread the thought of the van outside the house, the packing, the weariness of it all. A lot depends on whether we are moving to the unknown.

Jesus once talked about death as our final move to our last home. For us that means facing the unknown. But not for him.

> Do not let your hearts be troubled. Trust in God; trust also in me. In my Father's house are many rooms; if it were not so, I would have told you. I am going there to prepare a place for you. And if I go and prepare a place for you, I will come back and take you to be with me that you also may be where I am.
>
> John 14: 1–3

This passage speaks of Jesus' ascension to heaven. He was as familiar with heaven as we are with home. Jesus had moved from home when he came to this world, and speaks of going back there. He wasn't 'departing this life', destination unknown. He spoke from knowledge, without uncertainty or dread. He was going home to the Father's house and he wants us to trust him to make it a move we, too, need not dread.

What a contrast the certainty of Jesus is to everyone else. Shakespeare often expresses the most awful uncertainty: 'Ay, but to die and go we know not where.'

Many a modern finds our ignorance offensive:

> Life has no meaning,
> > but a struggling through the gloom,
> And the senseless end of it is
> > the insult of the tomb.

Our ascended Lord spoke differently when on earth for the simple reason that he alone is a witness. He has experience of heaven.

'I tell you about what I have seen in the Father's presence. I came from God and now I am here. You are of this world, I am not of this world, I came from above.' When there is only one eye-witness of the truth, it's crucial to believe him.

When Jesus speaks of 'my Father's house' he wants us to see that, for the person who trusts him, eternity is home. Think of the deep emotive phrases that gather round the place called 'home' when relationships are right and home means commitment, loyalty, and love.

'There's no place like home.' 'Welcome home.' 'You made me feel at home.' 'Home for Christmas.'

What those familiar phrases show is that something has gone terribly wrong when 'home is where the hate is,' the last place you want to be, when you have no home because it's broken up or because you have left, like the girl in the Beatles song, 'because she had lived alone for so many years,' a total stranger to her parents.

Human sin wrecks relationships. Homelessness is a deeper problem than too few houses. If every broken marriage, every teenager thrown out on his ear, every person abandoned by their family, could find a welcome back, homelessness would shrink.

It takes a lot to make that phone call that says, 'I'm sorry, please can I come home'. We need first to put our faith on the line and call on Jesus. He is the way back to the Father's home. He always welcomes and never rejects. He helps take away the hurt of others' rejection and encourages you to receive and forgive them. When he says, 'I'm preparing your room,' can you see he means it? It's as definite as that— booked, it's your place, no evictions or notices to quit, no raging rows, but forgiveness and welcome.

The Road Home

The nature of this exciting but unpredictable world gives no security. We all have enough terrible reminders of that. Yet the ascension of Jesus leaves the Christian in a 'no lose' position. The world we live in and can enjoy as God's creation we are also travelling through, on a journey to heaven, heading for home. Our permanent securities are there. So we set our sights higher than the things around us:

> Since, then, you have been raised with Christ set your hearts on things above, where Christ is seated at the right hand of God. Set your minds on things above, not on earthly things.

Col 3: 1–2

Because our generation is so sceptical about 'heaven and all that' we compensate by expecting the things of this life to satisfy. Just think how our home makes us the centre of the world. We expect it to shelter, warm, relax, and dignify us, to encompass us with soft music and interesting diversions, to be a theatre, a bar, the playground where our spouse has the soap opera glow of year round sun tan.

We expect more from this world alone than it was ever created to provide us with.

So we dig our pit of disillusion and then fall in. Like that guy in the film whose marriage has become a bore. He lives well enough and every morning his wife would ask him to empty the dustbin. That bin seemed to represent the week in week out, duty bound drudgery of marriage. He starts an affair. Every furtive meeting goes marvellously, until the time he first spent a night in her flat. As he left for work she says, 'O you wouldn't mind taking the dustbin out, would you?'

Ironically, if this life is all there is, we ourselves are just dust, and the ash heap is our destiny too. What a different dimension these studies give us.

A Christian has shared spiritually in a resurrection and ascension. He has been raised to new life with Christ, and so can set his heart on what Christ has for him. Thankfully, while we are on the journey home, God often satisfies us with all kinds of refreshment, with friends, gorgeous scenery and even hints in the sunrise and sunsets of the glory to come. But he will not allow us to mistake the joys on the way home, for home itself. So a Christian has a twofold outlook. He looks out on daily life and sees it as everyone else sees it, yet at the same time differently. He too has the dustbins to clear, and sees loved ones return to the dust. But the Christian also hears the words, 'To depart and be with Christ is far better.' We are not just dust, and life in Christ does not end on the ash heap.

To travel this road home in the company of others, to know where you are going, means you know what you live for, it transforms how you live. *Pilgrim's Progress* reminds us there are friends on this road to the Heavenly City called Honesty, Good Conscience, Mercy, Valiant for Truth, Faithful, Goodwill. Team up with that sort and we never walk alone.

But a generation that never takes that road loses touch with such friends. Home and community suffer. It does not pull together, stay together, or pray together. Are we entering a new Dark Ages of the spirit in the West? We may have more than enough to live on, but our crisis is, have we anything at all to live for, except the way of our dustbin hating husband—self satisfying pleasure as a way out of boredom—and no escape to happiness even then? Christians in the East see us as the deprived, and ask, 'Can the West be saved?'

Upwardly Mobile

Monty Python describes Christians as sycophants who spend their time 'buttering up God', trying to please him so he will give them something, like a master gives titbits to an obedient dog. Well, Monty's good at caricature and there are people who think that way.

But that's not Christianity. The real thing is about gratitude to God for what he has already given. Like the gratitude you'd feel towards someone who you had opposed and insulted, yet who turned up one day to say he'd written off all your debts and would love you to accept a house in the country. It made a new man of Paul:

> Set your minds on things above, not on earthly things.
> For you died, and your life is hid with Christ in God.

> When Christ, who is your life, appears, then you also
> will appear with him in glory.

Col 3: 1–4

The thrust of these words is—because we owe everything to Christ, we want to maintain close relationships with him. He's made a new man of me. So I want to please him. There's no hint of toadying. The effect of seeking the ascended Christ is to make the Christian upwardly mobile. Not to be a social climber (where I suspect buttering up is oft to be found), but to have the uplifting desire and discipline to rise above the current selfishness and cynicism; to ascend the hill of the Lord, with clean hands and a pure heart, but without arrogance, vanity, or deceit. Why does a man want to please Christ in this way?

1. Because we owe our new life to him. He 'is our life.' Physical and intellectual life are common to us all, but the gift of eternal life he gives to those who come to him. Without him we neither have it nor understand it, as the caricature shows.
2. Our life is rooted in his historical resurrection—a dead Christ could not impart life to anyone.
3. We want our life to reveal something of his. Because the risen Christ has ascended to heaven, his life is unseen. And so, in one sense, is the life he gives us. Real worship is of the heart. The flow of commuters cannot see the faith and joy you have in Christ, or the moral problems you pray through with him as you travel to work. Meditation is invisible, not, incidentally, because we look down into our hidden depths to try and find God there, but because we relate by faith to our ascended Lord. But, as it's impossible to set your mind on Christ and on sin at the same time, the effect Christ has on your actions, your character, your day to day affairs, is bound to show.

It shows when you refuse to get caught up in the constant craving and greed for more and hang the consequences. It shows in the battle for honesty, in the consistency of your marriage when your partner is not around, in the integrity of your work when others are on the skive. It'll show because you'll seek to be a better workmate, surgeon, businessman, husband, wife, employer, if you are a Christ-centred person. Colossians 3 is concerned that the heavenly dimension shows in the genuine ring to your life.

Sometimes the invisible life of Christ is made known through you, and the other guy begins to want it too.

The Unseen Control Centre

Ascension Day turns the world the right way up.

Scattered around the world are countless underground command posts, centres of nuclear power and control of chilling potential, all hid from our eyes. But there's another unseen control centre. The ascension of Jesus has both awesome and reassuring implications for where the ultimate control of our threatened, tattered planet lies.

> When I consider your heavens,
> The moon and the stars
> which you have set in place,
> What is man that you are mindful of him?
> You made him
> a little lower than the angels:
> You crowned him with glory and honour
> and put everything under his feet.
>
> Yet at present we do not see everything
> subject to him. But we see Jesus...now
> crowned with glory and honour because
> he suffered death...for everyone.
>
> Ps. 8: 3–5; Heb 2: 7–9

Imagine we could visit the high command control centre behind the universe. A huge screen shows all the thousands of galaxies. Buried amidst them we eventually find our own, in it we discover one ordinary star, our sun. Around it circles a minute dot—our earth.

When I consider the heavens—interstellar space—what is man? Who are we? In such impersonal vastness it seems that our meaning dies. We often feel that way. We have curved in on ourselves. Billions living in cities never look up to see a star, let alone the glory of God, the heavens glared out by sodium lights in the man-made streets.

But there's another map in that heavenly control centre. This one depicts not the vastness of space. It shows us the purpose behind the universe. So, on this map the earth is central. For this is where the destiny of God's special creation—man and woman—is being worked out.

It shows more than that. It is the planet God himself visited to rescue us from the trouble we had hurled ourselves into through sin. Jesus came, lived, died, rose again, and ascended in glory. 'All power is given to me, in heaven and earth,' he told his disciples on the day he left.

The Bible has its own way of speaking about heaven. What we call the atmosphere and ozone layer, the Bible calls the first heaven. What we call interstellar space it calls the second heaven. That's all visible.

But it also speaks of the third heaven, the heavenlies, which means the invisible, eternal world. No less real, it is the realm where God manifests his presence and glory, the place of high command, the control centre, invisible to us. That is where the Lord Jesus, after suffering death for everyone, dwells in his body of glory and honour.

This resurrection body of Jesus possessed a life which has its own new nature and powers. His ascension, witnessed by hundreds of disciples, specifically demonstrates that. He was going, he said, to prepare a place for us. He is preparing the new creation which will provide the environment and conditions for his glorified humanity, and in him, for ours too. 'There's a remaking ahead,' says C. S. Lewis. 'The old field of space, time, matter, and the senses is to be weeded, dug and sown by God for a new crop.'

Thrilling isn't it? Yet puzzling because of the lack of linkage—the discrepancy we all feel between 'heaven' and bodily life. This is a symptom of a much bigger problem. It's a symptom of the quarrel between man and God, the fracture between the natural world and the spiritual world, between heaven and earth. It is precisely one of the disorders Christ's new creation will come to heal. There's no permanent healing anywhere without it.

20

Pentecost Power

The Birth of the Church

Why did the church begin? Any castaway on a desert island who had a Bible could answer that question. 'Christians are people of a book,' said last month's issue of the journal, *History Today*. 'Christian origins can only be studied by reference to that book.'

And so, to find out why the church began, we read the Bible. The book itself, of course, begins with God. And it is intensely relevant to our question that we read also of dimensions that are also cosmic—the beginnings of the universe and life, and the beginnings of much else. Of man and marriage, of work and recreation, of sin and death, of pain and suffering, of breakdown of home and in society, of civilisation's roots and salvation's first glimmer. We see man in personal guilt 'Adam where are you?' and social guilt 'Cain, where is thy brother?' And it's all within the context of cosmic conflict, with the arch enemy of God contending for the prime target of God's creation—mankind. The personal, the social, the cosmic. In each area the taint of evil has blighted God's greatest good.

And so God has to make a new beginning which has in view the restored perfection of the created order.

And that's where the church comes in.

It began in order to bring God's message to a ravaged world. That message centres in the meaning of the death, resurrection, and ascension of God's son, Jesus Christ. It marks God's rescue of man from sin and death, his rescue of creation from its bondage to decay. With that small bunch of disciples in Jerusalem lay the key to the destiny of both the individual and the cosmos. God was launching the church—the new man in Christ, the new humanity that would first form the new society of Jesus in this world and which would ultimately inhabit the new heaven and the new earth. God gave the church to the world for many reasons. Let's look at some from Acts 2: 14–42, which tells of the church's beginnings:

The first was to communicate with people. Peter addressed the 'crowd'. There is a communication breakdown between God and the people of the world. Just think of the turbulent sea of sin and need that any crowd represents. Jesus saw the crowds and had compassion on them. Peter saw the crowd and proclaimed Jesus to them. He got through to people—Asians, Africans, Arabs, and Europeans. When the Holy Spirit gave his life-giving touch to the church, the church got in touch with people. The church began in order to bring Christ to the crowds and the crowds to Christ. Contact was established. Not just with any anonymous crowd, but with the individual in the crowd. Praise God, crowds still mass in places the world over when people are put in touch with God. But what do they need?

They needed an explanation of what life's all about. 'Let me explain what has happened,' Peter says. When you are puzzled and in the dark it's a mighty relief to have things explained. 'In this strange confusion, chaos or illusion, people seem to lose their way. Nothing left to strive for, love or keep alive for.' If you feel like that, let me explain to you, says Peter, that the basic meaning in life is found in what this wonderful person Jesus came to do for you. History is not sound and fury signifying nothing. We have just seen the fulfilment of the promises of God down through the centuries that he would bless all the nations of the world. Despite Lessing's ditch and Toynbee's stumbling block of particularity, the fact Jesus has come and gone has made all the difference to the world.

Jesus' resurrection has reversed the tyranny of death. The church began with a great birth cry, 'Jesus is risen.' 'Know this for sure,' says Peter in the church's first public utterance, 'God raised Jesus from the dead, freeing him from the grip of death, because it was impossible for death to hold on to him.' We are all witnesses to that fact. No resurrection, no message; no message, no church; no church, no meaning to life.

This life is not the only life. The early church lived on and lived out the gospel message of Jesus and the resurrection. It exists still to call us to faith in a risen Saviour for the forgiveness of sins. Unless the church projects that with the Holy Spirit's power, meaning drains away from the life of the individual and so too in the end does morality. No generation has witnessed this more than ours:

> Life has no meaning
> Just a struggling through the gloom
> And the senseless end of it
> Is the insult of the tomb.

Only the message of the empty tomb of Christ has the dynamic to wipe out that insult. The transformed disciples are themselves the best proof of that. And it convinced a cynical, sceptical, life weary age.

The crisis of our age is the belief that this life is the only life. Man has declared his origins, his beliefs, his loves to be but the outcome of an accidental collocation of atoms. We have reduced ourselves to a number of unrelated functions, so we can tell what we are, but not who we are. It is as if we can describe all the colours of the spectrum but have lost light itself to live by. That light comes through Christ the vanquisher of death. The church is not here to march men off to the king of terrors to the sound of the Dead March, but to the exhilarating notes of 'I know that my Redeemer liveth.'

In some ways, what happens next in the story of the church's beginnings shows us the most important of all the reasons for the church being here on earth. It's most important for me and you personally at least. The people, we read, 'were cut to the heart'. The church is here to awaken our consciences to our accountability before God. I may be quite happy that life is a random drift, that death is the end of everything and so I can live as I like. No one will call me to account. But the reverse side to resurrection and heaven is judgement and condemnation. When the meaning for life is grounded in eternity, then mortality takes on a new urgency. Just doing my own thing may, in fact, be doing a very dangerous thing. And so people were alarmed at Peter's sermon:

'What shall we do?'

The church is here to expose our sense of wrongdoing, to alert us to the judgement, to remind me that what I do now I shall be held accountable for then. From Herod to Hitler, from me to you.

When the message of the church assails the conscience, its own conscience included, it is fulfilling its original task. Without that, eventually and ominously, life and morality tend to part company. And so, when this crowd were galvanized into a conviction that they were far from being right with God, a most marvellous and healthy thing was happening. What?

The early church was coming into its own. It did what it was here to do. It offered the world a free gift. 'Repent, your sins will be forgiven in the name of Jesus. You will receive the gift of the Holy Spirit.'

Above all else, the church is the bearer of good news. God freely forgives us for Jesus' sake. He gives us eternal life through Jesus. In that crowd of hearers, as in your crowd and mine, were people who were suffering, guilty, violent, despairing, apathetic, self righteous, selfish, at odds with themselves and others.

They were made to see God loved them, Jesus had died for them. They received the message. They accepted the gift and to the church were added three thousand of such people. But they were now new people, Christ's people. They had begun a life of knowing and loving God. And wherever and whenever it happens, the church on earth is itself renewed and begins again, through them, to pass on its message of salvation to each lost generation. For that gift is for us too—'the promise is for you and your children and for all who are afar off.'

And so the issue is clarified. The church's task is to call on men to 'save themselves from this perverse generation' Are we just a product of our generation? Or are we people of God? To become a man of God is to become a servant of God, and then, in a new way, a servant of your generation. The closing picture of the young church in life and action shows something of the thrill of belonging to the people of God.

If the church is here on earth to declare by word the difference between God's way and man's, it is also here to embody in its life the contrast between God's way and man's. The new man in Christ, bound ultimately for the new heaven and earth, is to display now a new beauty of community. The early church, though not perfect, radiated a joy in worship and a beauty of relationships that gave the observer the plainest argument that this was not just men at work. The spontaneous and generous sharing of possessions was a prophetic challenge to injustice. It showed a turning from the world's life style to a serving of its life needs. It was a love demo of sacrificial living and it mediated the Saviour's dying love.

The church on earth can do no more, but we consistently offer so much less.

Living the Life

21

I'll Fear No Evil

Over the Easter period some years ago the entertainment world lost two great comedians—laughter makers. Laughter is a good medicine, says the Bible, yet in the end, faced with the end, every medicine fails, even for the laughter makers. One of them was afraid of the end, and sought help from those who cared for him.

How does the Easter message help us here? In whose hands are we in the end—after modern medicine has done its welcome best I mean? We often say, 'Good health—that's the main thing.'

Yet is it? The Easter message is that God's gift of eternal life in the risen Jesus is greater than even the gift of health. Sometimes, when health is threatened, belief in a risen Saviour gives a wholeness that shines out in people.

It showed recently in someone at the Royal Marsden Hospital, who I'll call Jenny.

After the trauma of several cancer operations, the surgeon said she needed yet another. The concern in his voice and eyes were so evident that Jenny reassured him. He must not worry: her cancer was not his fault, she could face it. 'You are the first patient that has ever tried to comfort me,' said the consultant, cupping her cheeks in his hands. As she left, the Outpatients Sister asked, 'Are you sure you're all right?' 'Yes thanks. I'm in God's hands.' The sister was delighted at her quiet faith. 'I'm a Christian too', she said and they made such a celebration over it, that the consultant overheard and said 'So am I.'

The day of the operation Jenny went to have a bath. She took her Bible with her, put it on the soap rack and it fell open at Psalm 34 :4. 'I sought the Lord and he answered me; he delivered me from all my fears. Those who look to him are radiant.' It gave her such reassurance that something of that radiance shone in her face. The ward Sister noticed the change in her and asked, 'What's happened to you?' 'I've had a bath,' she grinned.

Then who should turn up but the Outpatients Sister, who whispered in Jenny's ear: 'I sought the Lord, and he delivered me from all my fears.' She went to the theatre with the inner strength the Risen Lord can give as we face the unknown.

When she came round, a nurse said, 'There's some cards for you. Do you want to read them now?' 'O the top one's from my sister,' said Jenny, still groggy but recognizing the writing: 'Just that one.' The card had a verse on it. For the third time it was Psalm 34: 'I sought him and he delivered me.'

Jenny still enjoys the measure of health a successful operation brings. But she knows that part of being at peace with God is the knowledge that his final deliverance is still to come—that we are totally healed only on the other side of death.

The Easter message is that God raised Jesus from the dead, and because he lives, we shall live also. As we need our health to be in safe hands, so we need to put our life into his hands. A patient who can console a surgeon before a major operation, as Jenny did, is in the hands of Someone greater than he.

22

Michael Faraday—
Science and Christianity

Public assumptions are that science has discredited
Christianity. So when some of the greatest scientists who
happened also to be committed Christians receive public
attention, it's worth using the opportunity to show it is
a false assumption. For example, for many years the face of
Michael Faraday experimenting with electricity at the Royal
Institution appeared on the twenty pound note. Science
Museum posters in London saluted 'Faraday—The Father
of electricity—the man who changed the way we live.'

He certainly did that. What quick conveniences we owe
to him—microwave ovens for a start. He was possibly
the greatest experimental scientist ever. He electrified the
world, turned night into day and gave muscle and nerve
to our technology. Always pioneering ahead of his time, he
was constantly asked: 'What's the use of your experiments?'
'What's the use of a baby?' he would reply, 'Some day it will
grow up.'

Well, Faraday's science has grown up and it's turned us
into moderns. But are we growing up? Our abuse of science
hardly testifies to our maturity. Faraday knew well how
man's failure to grow up morally twisted every scientific
progress. His answer to that problem was unequivocal—
Christ.

Every Sunday he preached about him. His famous atheist colleague, Tyndall, marvelled at the intellectual strength Faraday derived from his 'Sunday exercises'—and he didn't mean jogging. Fellow scientists turned up to hear his refreshing sermons, drawn by the sheer goodness of the man, for Faraday was no religious fake

They heard him declare the Bible's message that God was his Creator and Christ his Saviour. Unlike, for example, Stephen Hawkins today, Faraday believed we can never find the meaning of life in the universe by reasoning from the natural world itself. That meaning comes through believing the testimony of God the Creator in Scripture. The Bible told him the earth is the Lord's. Science was the means of studying his handiwork. But he also believed our radical enemy is sin, our one hope is salvation in Christ. Without him, man fails to grow up to maturity and can turn all his gifts, science included, to selfish ends and spoil God's handiwork.

How wisely we use Faraday's scientific legacy depends much on how well we know the God he served as the Lord of Creation, life, and death. But because he knew the Lord his scientific legacy is not his only one. We benefit from science only until the moment we die. And what then? As his own end drew near his testimony shines with a different light than electricity affords. May they lighten our darkness:

> My earthly faculties are slipping away. Happily, the true good does not lie in them. As they ebb, may they leave us all as little children, trusting in the Father of mercies and accepting his unspeakable gift of life in his beloved Son. Peace is the gift of God alone; and as it is he who gives it, why should we be afraid?

23

Green Things

Though many former industrial areas are green again, Earth Summits have grimmer things to consider. You've got to hand it to those pop prophets of the sixties. Some of their throbbing themes have caught up with the rest of us:

> What have they done to the earth?
> What have they done to our fair sister?
> Ravaged and plundered
>   And ripped her and bit her.

Years ago, an American worried at pollution levels, set up a tombstone down by the ocean and carved this epitaph:

> Once the oceans were born...
>   The Lord gave
> The oceans died AD 1999.
>   Man hath taken away....

Doomwatch exaggerations apart, mankind has bungled the tenancy the Lord gave us of land, sea, and ozone layer. We've reneged on the tenancy agreement. We've not held the estate as good stewards from him. The estate's potential for shelter and provision has declined through thoughtless greed.

Some climate and conservation scientists say we need, therefore, to be reconciled to the Creator as well as nature. Some Christians in science are helping to set the agenda. For example, the Director of Kew Royal Botanic Gardens,

Professor Prance, an authority on the Amazonian rain forest, puts the need of reconciliation this way:

'It was at Oxford University that I first made a firm commitment to the Christian faith and the teaching of the Bible and accepted Christ. The biblical command in Genesis to serve and preserve the earth, began to take on a new meaning to me.' The Bible speaks of 'God the Father's good pleasure to reconcile all things to Himself through Christ, whether things on earth, or things in heaven, having made peace through the blood of his cross'. Dr Prance goes on to say that 'those who are reconciled to God in Christ are also reconciled to his creation, and the only chance of survival for that creation is if those who are reconciled defend it.'

The former Director General of the Met Office and Chairman of the International Panel on Climate Change is Professor Houghton, an old boy of Rhyl Grammar school in North Wales. He also interweaves faith and science:

'The Jesus I meet in the Gospels is the One I know in personal experience as I attempt to communicate with God in prayer. He also enables the two strands of my life as scientist and Christian to be brought together side by side.' As a scientist, he finds the personal God of the Bible big enough—big enough to be behind the Big Bang, if such it was. And alongside that, as a Christian believer, he found God personally close enough to give his wife, dying of cancer at 54, a strong and radiant faith in the resurrected Christ and the conviction that life does not fade away into nothingness.

If we were just of the earth, and there were no Creator, we would be bound for nothingness, and the planet we inhabit would orbit impersonally on without us. But God in Christ is big enough to have made us for eternity. Meanwhile, he has put the earth in our hands. As tenants, Drs Prance and Houghton are among those serving the Lord, and us, in taking responsible care of his estate.

Mind you, it's still difficult to believe the danger when I look out of my window towards the Brecon Beacons National Park, but then it's also difficult to believe the wayside text, 'Prepare to meet thy God,' when we pass with our car full of petrol and our lives full of fun.

24

Fatherly Care

Have you seen the car sticker: 'Caution—child in back; Beware—father in front.' A bit blunt, but it showed a dad at the wheel who cared for his children. Many fathers do the opposite these days—abandoning family ties, leaving their children, even leaving them without means of support. Is that what you'd expect from a father? Fathers know how to give good things to their children, says Jesus in Luke 11. Of course. But, almost in the same breath, he identifies why fatherhood can be flawed by selfish hardheartedness:

> Which of you fathers, if your son asks for a fish, will give him a snake instead? Or if he asks for an egg, will give him a scorpion? If you then, though you are evil, know how to give good gifts to your children, how much more will your Father in heaven give the Holy Spirit to those who ask him.
>
> Luke 11: 11–13

The parallel Jesus is drawing is based on the expectation that fatherly care will prevail even over the evil bent of our nature. Which of you fathers would let his child come down to breakfast this morning, and give him sand in place of cornflakes? Would a father have such cynical disregard for his children? Jesus asserts our essential sinfulness clearly enough, but he also asserts that normal fathering is made of the stuff that counteracts the selfishness we know we are capable of. The stability of life is built on such parenting.

This homely illustration exposes the present family scene. The flight of fathers from the home reflects the decline of normal God-given duties and joys. There have always been bad fathers and there have always been children dreadfully under threat from them. But now the practise of fatherhood itself is becoming dispensable. The absent father, indifferent to the existence of his own children, not there even to be asked for good things, is a sad deviation. It is one of the moral and family shadows of sex without responsibility, a dividing of what God has joined. The evil flaw in our nature, taking advantage, as it always will, of social tendencies, is gaining ground.

Can it be countered? Has Jesus anything to tell us about that? He has. He says our heavenly Father is eager to give the Holy Spirit to them who ask. Jesus always goes to the root problem. The Spirit of God is the only good gift powerful enough in this world to change these awful tendencies in the human heart. So ask. Be persistent, urgent for him to come—'Ask…seek…knock', says Jesus. The Holy Spirit of God is indispensable to convince us we must one day answer to God for how we live. The history of spiritual revival in our land demonstrates how God stops the rot in man's heart and stays the decline of a generation. His Spirit can give us new life and turn us into people and parents, who, though far from perfect, begin to reflect the grace and discipline of our merciful Father in heaven.

What a prospect!

Sad homes tasting again the joy and blessing of men who know and show what being a dad is all about. And what if there's no father at the wheel any more? Even then Jesus came to show us there is Someone there to care—a loving heavenly Father who hears the cry of the fatherless, hurt by life's stones and scorpions. We can enter a real relationship of trust in him, where the perfect love of Jesus casts out fear. And Jesus, let's not forget, says 'Beware' to those who endanger 'little ones' in life's traffic, and cause them to stumble maimed through life's journey.

The Prayer for Today

The best known prayer is the Lord's Prayer. Rattling it off in school assembly was a bit like talking to ourselves aloud. If human beings are just complex cogs whirring away in a mechanistic universe such monologue is all you can expect. But God is there, and real prayer, says Jesus, is dialogue with someone we can relate to personally, none other than 'Our Father in heaven.'

This is how you should pray: 'Our Father in heaven, hallowed be your name, your kingdom come, your will be done on earth as it is in heaven' (Matt. 6: 9–10).

The existence of the Lord's Prayer raises a great question. Is there anyone to pray to, or do we settle for the idea that prayer is a help for certain types, just as meditation or aerobics or jogging is helpful for others?—just a way of talking to yourself that helps you tidy yourself up, like looking in a mirror. The mirror, of course, helps you to do that, but nobody deceives himself into thinking there's anybody there in the mirror. Turn away and there's only you.

Well, is there only you? Prayer can be a babble of self deception. Jesus plainly tells us so. But to those who think it's never anything but a monologue, Jesus is saying God is there to get to know. As we go out today into the baffling, sometimes cruel world of events and circumstances, the riddle of life confronts us like a heavy curtain. Behind that curtain stands God, the Father Almighty, Creator of heaven and earth. Your heart-cries, your deep questions need not be a monologue. They can be part of a dialogue with him, which is what true prayer is.

Of course, we may have attitudes poles apart from prayer as we stand before the curtain. We may stand there bewildered, trying to fathom things out, wondering if the mystery will ever be solved. You may stand there with clenched fists, angry with whoever seems to be responsible for it all, or mocking the idea there could be anyone there.

Yet God will not be banished even in our mocking. All those attitudes show we cannot escape from relating to him somehow. If we will not talk with God, we talk to ourselves—the self God the Creator gives us. That self throws back at me all the questions I cannot answer without him. That really is standing before a mirror, looking at ourselves and no further, looking at humanity as ultimate. We cannot even find ourselves that way, for God has made us for himself, and God is no mirror image of us.

Life is a riddle and honesty testifies that prayer is meaningless unless we know God as Father. But it is no pointless question to stand today before the mystery curtain and ask, 'Is there anybody there?' Jesus bids us come to the Father who is there behind the curtain. God is not just a hidden Listener, he speaks to us through his Son. The invisible God is not unknown, for in Jesus we meet someone who came this side of the curtain awhile and came to show us the Father. In him we find God and in him we become children of God and find our true self. One day the curtain will finally rise and we shall see, face to face, Jesus, the Resurrection and the Life, the eternal Son who is the way to the Father.

Praying for Bread

If I asked you to jot down now the three most important needs in your life, what would they be? In the Lord's Prayer, Jesus gives us the three priorities for living that we most need to get in touch with God about:

> 'Give us today our daily bread. Forgive us our debts, as we also have forgiven our debtors. And lead us not into temptation, but deliver us from evil.' For if you forgive men when they sin against you, your heavenly Father will also forgive you. But if you do not forgive men their sins, your Father will not forgive your sins.
>
> Mat 6: 11–15

Here are the basics of our moral and spiritual well-being: bread for today, forgiveness for the sins of yesterday, and protection from any future evil. Let's look at the prayer for bread, and for protection from evil, for evil often denies people bread.

The prayer for daily bread is a subtle phrase that means: 'Give us today what we need for tomorrow.' We know how much easier it is to live less anxiously if tomorrow's needs are looked after today. But Jesus is opening our eyes to more than merely our own good. 'Give us our daily bread,' says our Lord—not, 'Give me'. This kind of dependence upon God helps us bear in mind the anxieties of others who have less than us. Sharing what I have is God's means of answering their prayer, showing them he is still in touch.

For example, people are now able to go freely to Eastern Europe with vanloads of necessities. Some had brought occasional supplies for years, though secretly, because of danger. Because evil strangled the provision of many necessities, people prayed much for deliverance. In life's battle with the colossus of evil, prayer is a line of communication with God. 'You do your worst, we shall do our best,' said Churchill to the enemy. In the spiritual battle, our best at all times is prayer that gets through to God.

Think of it this way. You live in a far off place where an enemy is making life difficult for you. You send a message to those back home—you need clothes, food, medicine. You wait. Then a package comes.

Its arrival makes you happy for two reasons: first, you know your message has got through—an answer proves there is love and care for you. Secondly, you now have some of the things you needed. The 'things' won't last long, but the fact you are in touch means someone is there to help.

So, when deprived and stressed Christians have asked God for necessities, answered prayer does not just make them grateful for 'things', it thrills them to know they are in touch with him, even though every influence about them denies his existence.

As we help them with material things, we see what trial has done for them—what Christian character and endurance it has yielded, what delight in the Lord Jesus when all was drab and despairing, what confirming of faith when deliverance has come. A recent letter from our Romanian church link said—read Psalm 126. We did. 'Our tongues were filled with songs of joy. Then it was said among the nations, "The Lord has done great things for them." The Lord has done great things for us and we are glad.'

We who have both 'things' and freedom can humbly rejoice that days of refining fire have given them a purer gold of faith to enrich us all.

Forgiveness

'Christianity asserts that every human being is going to live for ever. This must be either true or false. Now many things would not be worth bothering about if I were going to live only seventy years. ' C. S. Lewis continues, 'If I am going to live for ever I had better bother about them very seriously. Perhaps my angry temper is only gradually getting worse— not so noticeably maybe over my seventy years or so. But it would be absolute hell in a million years: in fact, if Christianity is true, hell is precisely the correct technical term for what it would be.'

Compare what Jesus says in the Sermon on the Mount:

> I tell you that anyone who is angry with his brother will be subject to judgement. Again…anyone who says 'You fool' will be in danger of the fire of hell. Therefore, if you are offering your gift at the altar and remember that your brother has something against you, leave the gift there in front of the altar. First go and be reconciled to your brother.
>
> Mat 5: 22–24a

Now, if God were but an invention, religion only empty ritual, if our seventy years ended everything, we could bother as little about attitudes of anger and contempt as this angry fellow Jesus is describing.

But Jesus bothers a great deal. Our darker thoughts are under God's judgement: not only because they are like hugging high explosives in the mind which can give rise to actual murder: they are, in themselves, culpable in the sight of God. For what we are in our hearts now, we are not only at risk of becoming in our actions, but we shall increasingly be for all eternity.

These attitudes that build inside us over our seventy years, distancing us from people with whom we've fallen out, leave us unreconciled both to God and man.

In the Lord's Prayer Jesus opens for us the road to reconciliation. 'Forgive us our trespasses as we forgive them who trespass against us.' When God grants us the forgiveness we seek of him, he insists we show ourselves ready to forgive others.

Forgiving others is a basic human necessity. Yet our pride seems impotent to give it, until pride is broken as we pray for forgiveness ourselves. When we do, the joy of knowing God's forgiveness of our own sin has a power about it that breaks our hardness. We pass on that forgiveness, as did an estranged couple, who were brought together again by a recent broadcast sermon, and their joy knew no bounds, or like that Korean pastor did, when he forgave and adopted into his own family the young communist who had murdered his only son.

Dynamic changes occur when we are moved to forgive others because God has forgiven us. The God who is there to hear and deal with us transforms life's wrong attitudes. Such prayer is no illusion going on in our own head—a kind of private thought for the day—a spiritual aspirin that helps if life's a bit of a headache, making you feel better, just as music or flower arranging might.

No! Prayer for forgiveness of sin meets the supreme need of man, through the grace of God. Through Jesus, the Saviour from sin, we come into touch with the living God, who reads our unseen thoughts with penetrating scrutiny. To come to know his forgiving love is joy unspeakable, and in the end how can we do without it?

25

A Father's Welcome

A teacher recently asked a four-year-old girl if she knew any nursery rhymes. The little girl shook her head. Her teacher persisted, trying 'Ring-a-Ring o' Roses' and 'Baa, baa, black sheep.' No response.

The only songs she knew were the jingles from television adverts picked up during lonely hours of watching. This lack of what we now call 'parenting skills' has become a concern to the National Society for the Protection and Care of Children, because telling stories is not just fun, it also forges a vital bond between parent and child.

I remember the happy time when I started to tell Bible stories to my lad of three. One was about the boy who charged into his dad's room one day and shouted, 'Dad, I'm off! I can't stick it here any longer. But I want all the pocket money I can have—and I want it now. Now!' To his astonishment, his dad handed him a heavily laden piggy bank. 'I'll be back one day...perhaps,' the son called as he dashed out of the door.

He was soon into a prodigal spending spree. A trip to the cinema every day, new roller skates, a small fortune spent on ice creams, chocolate, and chewing gum. He had a great time at fairs and soon gathered a gang of guys around him.

By now my little boy's eyes were getting wider and wider. I'm sure you can guess the end of the story....before long he'd spent all the money in the piggy bank. Penniless, his gang deserted him. Even worse, he was starving, hungry, and absolutely famished. He thought of tea time with his mum and dad. Oh, if only he could go home.

In the end that's what he did, deciding he'd have to risk his father's anger, go back and try to say he was sorry.

As he neared home he began to feel scared. Perhaps his dad wouldn't take him back—he was so dirty for a start. By now my little boy and I were looking out of the window at our back gate. 'Do you know what happened?' I said, 'as he came up to the gate? His father saw him and rushed out to meet him. Instead of greeting him with angry words, he flung his arms around him, welcomed him home, and then...' but before I could finish the story, my lad flung his arms around my neck and gave me a great big hug.

The original story of course is not just about a wayward child. Jesus, in the parable of the Prodigal Son, is assuring all of us of the love and welcome of our heavenly Father when we return to him.

26

Self and Service

One of life's tasks is to balance true self fulfilment with service to others, says Herman Bavinck. As individuals, you and I have a created need of self expression—to be able to use our own gifts in a way that enables us to be ourselves. But whatever we find to give ourselves to, needs also to fit in with serving others. To put it succinctly—to exist is to serve. Without this, society falls apart.

We see this dependence on mutual service in nature where everything is dependent in one way or another. Plants need soil. Animals need plants. Each serves the other. Even the rotation of the earth is a service of major significance, for night and day make life possible. The interdependence of the inanimate world illustrates the Creator's purpose that every part of the creation should serve him and each other.

The big question for humanity is: Why is this not so with us, even after all the centuries of human endeavour? If this ideal of service could completely capture everyone's life, then humanity would be in a perfect situation.

The Bible's analysis is that we have a twist away from God—a biased inclination towards serving self as the centre of our world. We love self, rather than God.

It's not difficult to observe this bias at work in ourselves. We can watch someone in trouble and decide to draw away from them into ourselves rather than get involved. This is why God's command to 'Love your neighbour as yourself' is so profoundly intrusive. But it is not only intrusive. In some incredibly powerful way, it is the key to life as God intended it. We've all glimpsed that truth in our own experience. To give real pleasure to others by serving them is one of the true joys of existence. 'It is more blessed to give than to receive.' That's not just a Christmas delight.

This recognition that we are to serve others has a balancing side to it. I also need them to serve me. It's blessed to receive too. Unless I see others value me then my humanity shrivels. We all need appreciation to gain self respect. God has made us dependent on each other in this.

And yet, because we are so turned in on ourselves rather than on God, self esteem can also become an idol. For example, we may present a fine case for a good cause, something far higher than ourselves. We are totally in subjection to the noble cause we serve. But if someone else speaks even better about the same cause and gets more applause, we find that difficult. Why? The cause is still being served isn't it? Ah, but not me any longer, so I'm not so interested in the cause. I'm more interested in me.

Only in Jesus do we see total consistency. Self is not a problem to him. He is identified with the cause he came to serve. But notice, he did not come just to give an example of how selflessly to serve others. That would not win us from our self love. It's not possible to love someone else if his life at every point merely stands in judgement on our own, showing us up. If we're to love and serve him rather than self, we need to be freed from the bondage to self love.

And that's what begins to happen when we see that the way Jesus served us was to save us. He loves us as we are, with all our self serving bias and invites us to love and serve him not just for time but for eternity. It's there we find both self fulfilment and the motive to serve. The Apostle John sums it up: 'For if he so loved us, we ought also to love one another.'

27

Idle Days

'Why are you standing here idle all day?' someone asks a group of men at the street corner. 'Because no-one will employ us,' they reply. That's not a comment overheard in an ex-mining village. It's from one of Jesus' parables.

Enforced idleness, or life without work, never really goes away. The 1940s Beveridge Report declared that idleness caused by unemployment was the largest and fiercest giant post-war Britain faced.

Things have been worse, much worse, and have got better, much better, but one of the sad new trends is that, whereas once hardship tended to reinforce a family's will to pull together, now it's pulling couples apart. The young mother of fifty years ago, pushing her second hand carriage perambulator (remember them?), was very unlikely to swap husbands, have a series of boyfriends, or settle for being a single mum. But the chubby child in the baby buggy you'll see in the street today is at risk. Soon he may have no dad around or will have to get used to a stranger. Are the employed and unemployed young dads and mums of today intrinsically more heartless and nastier? Of course not. But most of them are now cut off from Christian roots and resources. The love and faithfulness they nourish are still the keys to pulling together when trouble strikes.

When a family find these keys, they are likely to open up much richer relationships than any welcome upturns in the economy. Example speaks louder than theory. So let me give you one. A young mother stood at our door— distraught. The night before, her husband, who'd had an upsetting stretch of unemployment, had hit her, thrown her to the floor, and kicked her about as the children screamed and pleaded for it to stop.

'The hopeless thing about it all' she said, 'is that he's never said "I'm sorry" in all our years together. I'm now terrified of more violence. Where can I get help?' My hand was on the phone when we decided that, first, we'd pray about what was the right thing to do. It changed everything. 'I'll make another go of it,' she said. Back home she put her arms around the children and prayed with them. She thanked the Lord for their dad, praying that his heart would be turned to love and not anger.

A little later, the children were doing their homework, tense, waiting for their father to come home. Then one of the boys said, 'Mummy, I'm not afraid anymore,' and when dad did come home they rushed to the door to meet him. His first words told them that the Lord had heard their cry. 'I'm sorry for what happened last night, love.' For the first time, he said it and meant it. From that time on they've all been learning to pull together.

Idleness and its hardships need not kill loyalty. In the midst of life without work perhaps the most important thing to learn is 'Don't just sit there, pray something.' This family cried and the Lord saved them…and delivered them from their distress.

28

Beating Inflation

Inflation hitting 10.9% is hardly a cause for thanksgiving. But the day those figures came out, I heard of a hard up elderly couple that has left me thinking 'thanksgiving' ever since. This couple turned up recently at the Birmingham City Mission with a gift and this story.

After years in poor housing, they had moved to a modern Council flat. They were told social security would rise to pay the rent. But heating costs soared and they got into debt. So they decided that each time they drew their pension they would dedicate it to God. Every Thursday, home from the Post Office, they put their money on the kitchen table, beside their bills, and prayed. As they handed in their gift to the Mission, they said, 'Since doing that we're out of debt. Here's a thank offering of last month's surplus.' What a response to a pension surplus: give thanks to God and give it away.

Isn't thanksgiving uplifting? Especially when it's thanks plus giving. People still attend Harvest Thanksgiving services. Its not hard to be thankful in our green and pleasant land. Such thanksgiving festivals also give us opportunities to add giving to thanks—our surplus to areas of chronic drought and famine.

Harvest Thanksgiving last year took a dramatic turn for me. On the way, a car coming out of a junction hit our car. We mounted the crash barrier, took off, hurtled airborne through a traffic sign, soft-landing on a grass central reservation. A near thing. The car was a write off. We didn't make the service. But we shared what I was going to speak on with the people who stopped to help. It was the parable about the guy who'd made a fortune out of farming and then just wanted to eat, drink and be merry. But God interrupted him, 'Fool, tonight your life will end. Then what?'

We had a close shave that night, and our instant reaction was, 'Thank you, Lord, we're still alive.' We're also thankful that the accident spot has now been made safe. That near miss produced a new junction and driving past now, we see how good can come out of trauma.

But there's another dimension of thanksgiving for the Christian. I don't want our reserve about death to make me shy to talk about it. I can't forget that parable. Every man's journey through life is finally interrupted. Can there be thanksgiving then? Yes. 'A Christian doesn't want to die,' said the late Lord Tonypandy, former speaker of the British House of Commons—'but he can look forward to heaven.'

Death is a spoilsport, an enemy that always wins. Isn't the ultimate statistic—one out of one dies? No! A greater fact breaks that deadly statistical pattern. 'One died for all' says the Bible, 'He died for our sakes and rose again.' Christ's resurrection means death does not win. 'O death, where is your victory? Thanks be to God. He gives us the victory through our Lord Jesus Christ.' God's supreme gift is eternal life, through Jesus Christ. So, receiving the gift is the supreme cause of thanksgiving.

That elderly couple have more than their surplus to thank God for as they pray around the kitchen table.

29

Holiday Abroad

When my wife and I were preparing to go off on holiday via Dover we heard on the radio about an absent minded professor. He too drove off on a continental holiday with his wife. When he got back home the police called:

'Are you Dr so and so?'

'Yes.'

'Well sir, you've left your wife at Dover.'

Such perils apart, we look forward to our holidays together. The word holiday comes, of course, from 'holyday'. Just as fun and faithfulness, joy and holiness, live together in Christian marriage, so holidays and the Christian life cohabit happily, for holidays are God's idea. He gave us one day in seven for rest and recreation and also encouraged his people in Old Testament times to take weeklong holiday festivals. They camped out, praised God with music, had celebration meals, and feasted on good Bible teaching. At one of those holiday camps, held after they'd completed a rebuilding programme to house the homeless, they were refreshed by God's blessing. They put it like this: 'The joy of the Lord is our strength.'

Joy is a tonic. When we're miserable nothing seems to go right, work or holidays. But what a difference when we're happy and especially when joy flows down from the Lord to us. Then we go through work like a knife through butter. And what's a holiday when joy is absent?

Of course, joy needs identifying. When a vicar closed his service with the words, 'Go out with joy,' a lad in the back seat muttered: 'Who's Joy?' Precisely. To know the joy of the Lord we have to come to know the Lord who gives it. The joy he gives strengthens everything that's good and lasting in life. The cheering factor in this is that every summer thousands of youngsters at Christian holiday camps find out about that joy. As they look at what the Bible says about life it often leads them to a new wholesome life style in Christ. It gives them a moral compass. It helps them value the integrity of girls and to turn away from the stolen 'joy ride' of the one night stand. It helps them see fun and faithfulness as life long friends and so produces better dads and husbands. That's a joy and a strength in itself.

It was even more cheering to have a card through the post from an international Christian camp in Austria. Students from thirty three nations tackling tough issues as wide as life itself—among them Serbs, Croats, Estonians, Romanians, Latvians, Poles, Chinese—all gathered to hear God's word for their situation, praying together for strength to face the challenges back home, relishing the joyous atmosphere that strengthens the will to transcend national strife and helps them persevere as servants of Christ. And all that on holiday, amidst the glories of the Austrian Alps.

It certainly makes us look forward to the holiday joy of the Lord…let's hope I keep my wits about me at Dover.

30

An Identity Crisis

In Wales and in countless Welsh Societies around the world, Welshness waves like daffodils and leeks, its national emblems, on 1 March, the day of its Patron Saint. School children participate in the Welsh language in cultural festivals called *eisteddfodau* where there are harps a plenty, and groups singing 'penillion'—a special Welsh 'sound'. Rousing male voice song fills Cardiff's St David's Hall. But Wales has an identity crisis. Wales today is losing its faith; there's a vacuum in our soul. The land of Song was also the land of the Book and Revival. Wales' most powerful poet, Williams Pantycelyn, whose bicentenary in 1991 was marked on Radio 2, was a hymn writer. He fired the hearts of a nation to sing of Jesus and his love. But 'Guide me O Thou Great Jehovah' lacks conviction when Wales play rugby these days—not just because we're losing matches, but because the men no longer know Pantycelyn's words. There's a vacuum in the valleys. We're missing those Bible Classes of miners and tinplate workers who turned Sunday afternoons into a kind of spiritual university, where the men faced life's big questions with open Bibles.

That's exactly what happened when Martyn Lloyd-Jones began to preach at Aberavon in the thirties. Talk among the dockers at the Working Men's Club soon centred round the conversions among their mates. Just three examples: One man, whose life seemed a hopeless wreck, overheard this remark: 'At that church last Sunday that preacher said nobody was hopeless.' So he went, and found rescue in Christ. Another vicious local character, who had cut his dog's head off with a carving knife because it had eaten his meal, turned up one Sunday and was saved instantly. He became a working class gentleman. In a local school, a boy beamed up at his teacher: 'We had dinner today, Miss. Gravy, potatoes, meat, cabbage, and rice pudding.' The reason followed: 'My father has been converted.' Up till then, Dad's wages had gone on drink.

This was no passing wonder. For thirty years at London's Westminster Chapel, Lloyd-Jones demonstrated, with the sharp, clinical diagnosis of a physician, that Christ alone answers our deepest needs. In science labs, boardrooms, medical schools, lecture rooms and pulpits you'll find people who found that answer through his preaching. The Word of God, proclaimed with logic, realism, and thrilling spiritual power, moved them from unbelief to the solid rock of Christ. He spoke heart to heart in critical days. In his famous broadcast message at the Cardiff Civic service during the Suez crisis, the programme well overran its time as the nation heard the alarm he sounded.

He was an international Christian figure and people overseas recognized in him the true Welsh spiritual heritage. But his burden was that Wales was losing it. He longed for revival. He knew a touch of it himself. For example, one day, while reading the hymns of Pantycelyn, God gave him a blazing consciousness of his love. God's presence became an overwhelming certainty and joy. Its impact came through at the National Eisteddfod at Dolgellau. At midnight he preached on 'Rejoice in the Lord,' to a great Noson Lawen (Joyful night) organized by Bangor University students. Next day the BBC reporter commented how preacher and students longed that Wales should emerge from her scepticism and materialism.

I share that longing. I'd love, of course, to see a revival of Welsh rugby tomorrow. Another Golden Era would lift us no end. But when God revives his work in our land that will restore the soul and identity of Wales.

31

Behind the Iron Curtain

We had arrived at the airport a few hours earlier, and now stood at the end of a queue, watching nervously as customs officers carried out thorough baggage searches. In our luggage were some Bible Study notes in the local language for some Eastern bloc university students we were visiting. Thankfully we were waved on, unsearched.

A friend and I had been invited to provide Christian teaching for these students and they'd done this despite the risk to themselves.

At 3 am I was wakened as the door of my hotel room swung open. A woman glanced round, looked in a fridge and then left. How odd! It turned out she was a security agent. Next day she broke her leg. This meant the authorities lost touch with us.

We easily forget how harsh restrictions were on freedom of worship in Iron Curtain days. Then, even our travel to the mountain hideaway had to be carefully inconspicuous. Once hidden in the forest, it was a thrill to preach from the Bible, through enthusiastic interpreters, to young men and women eager to know more of the gospel and to pray about God's will for their lives.

After supper we sang hymns round the camp fire. We began to feel safer and more relaxed. Some of us had retired to our tents for the night and were laughing loudly when... suddenly the singing stopped. A medical student came and urged us to be quiet. A car had just bumped its way up a forest path into the camp. The driver wore a peaked cap. It looked like trouble. There were a few anxious moments until he was recognized as a student arriving late. But the suspense brought home the risks Christians took to encourage each other.

On the way home, airport customs interrogated us closely. For some reason, the official was not satisfied. He locked the gate, told the rest of the queue to join another, put on his hat, and with gun in holster marched us away. Our hearts raced. A woman at a desk gave us a heavy fine. But then we were free to go.

As I sat in the plane I saw our luggage being trolleyed to the aircraft. I watched in horror as a pocket of my rucksack burst open and the notes of my talks blew across the tarmac. The driver gave chase and recovered them, unwittingly rescuing the sensitive material.

I'm glad he saved all my hard work, but even if the notes had blown away on the wind, their message would not have been lost. Those young students have stood the test and remain faithful servants of Jesus Christ.

32

The Bible—from Wales to Korea

When you recall the Christian influence of Welshmen across the world, few can surpass Robert Thomas who grew up in the village of Llanover, near where I live. His story tells how God can bring good out of tragedy. In 1863 Thomas set sail for China with his young wife. She and their child died only months after they arrived in Shanghai. Robert's conviction that Jesus was the Lord of life did not die, however, and he became the first man to take Bibles to Korea. He was killed as he set foot on Korean soil. Yet, out of that mission has come an astonishing resurrection, for the Korean Church has grown more quickly than any during this century. Many Koreans visit the chapel in Llanover, near Abergavenny where he was ordained.

I went there first with a pastor from Seoul. I shall not forget his gratitude to God as we looked at the commemorative plaque and the portrait of the young Welshman who brought the Christian gospel to his homeland.

The chapel itself snuggles close to the Llanover estate in South Wales. At the time Thomas was brought up there, the lord of the estate was Sir Benjamin Hall, commissioner of works when Big Ben, London's famous clock, was built and so named after him. Thomas, too, went off to London and became top linguist of his year at the University.

After meeting some Koreans in China, Thomas soon learned the language. As the only known European in China who could speak Korean, it got him on to an American trading ship as interpreter. His motive was purely one of bringing Bibles to the people. As the ship sailed up the river to Pyongyang he threw Bible portions ashore. They were read with effect. A Korean who later became a Christian said how his father had picked one up at Kang-suh-po-san. But the government understandably feared western imperialism and felt the ship's advance up river a threat—though nothing was further from Thomas' mind. When the ship was stranded on mud flats it was set alight. Thomas waded ashore in the shallow water, taking his Bibles with him. Everyone was executed as they landed, Thomas included.

My Korean friend told me what became of the Bibles. Apparently, children took some copies home, and their parents used the paper as wallpaper. Then they started to read their wallpaper. The message of God's love for the world, silenced on Thomas' lips, changed their lives. Others believed too and when American missionaries arrived twenty years later they found a dozen or more Koreans who shared the young Welshman's faith.

The Koreans have been called the 'Welsh of the east'. They certainly love hymn singing. Not long after the Welsh Revival of 1904, revival began at Pyonyang too. Churches sprang up where Thomas had died, and in modern South Korea one in four now share the Christian faith. Thomas is honoured as the one who brought the news of God's forgiveness in Christ.

So, little Llanover has left its mark. Big Ben, named after the local lord, is a symbol of reliable time keeping throughout the world. But I think of the text of the first message young Robert Thomas preached in Llanover chapel: 'Jesus Christ, the same yesterday, today and forever.' As we recall the sacrifice of yesterday of that lad of twenty-seven, let's 'Remember Jesus Christ, risen from the dead', the Lord of today and forever, who is also Lord of East and West, and whose gift of eternal life is for all nations.

33

The Love of Money

The old song says, 'Money is the root of all evil.' But the Bible targets the love of money. When we love money rather than God, the whole purpose of living suffers a distortion. We just want to have.

And money seems the most powerful of things people want to have. Money itself is a good, necessary, and powerful servant. But if we love money, it masters us. People will not only work for it, but steal, cheat, gamble, and kill for it. Its power over our lives is that of a substitute god. If we don't believe in the true God and are taken in by the view that this world is all there is, then this world's god—which is what Jesus calls money—holds power over us.

Why has money this power? asks Herman Bavinck

For one thing, it's a key—a key to something else. If you've a key in your pocket, it's a key to what we've already got—house, car. But money in our account is a key to what we haven't got—yet. Money can become anything. It's a ticket that opens the possibility of the luxury hotel, the gorgeous dress, the graceful yacht. This romance and temptation of money is also its trap, because the romance can bring disillusion. Things we buy with money eventually weary and leave us discontented (how long before the Christmas toy is cast aside?). But somehow money itself transcends this, because it is bewitching possibility—a dream of what could be.

Money also has power because it seems to put us into a different league and make us into another grade of person. Notice the difference between these statements—'He's good, he's wise, he's rich.' By the last we mean he has riches. It doesn't say anything about his personal quality. When we ask 'how much is he worth?' we mean 'how much has he got?' Yet we say he is rich. He gets status from his money. Anything that robs him of his money actually robs him of his importance. 'I'm ruined! I've lost everything,' he says. Sometimes the suicide that follows shows he meant it.

We all know deep down, though money can buy us all sorts of things, life is more than things money can buy. 'Money can't buy me love', sang the Beatles and I suppose they ought to know. Nor health, nor intelligence, nor happy marriages, nor inner joy…money can't buy any of these. And it conveys no moral force. In fact, as we know, it can wilt it. It's counterfeit when it comes to all this.

Yet somehow we prefer not to believe that. It's almost an unwritten law these days that we do not expose this god for what it is. But come into the company of Jesus, and we find that when he saw money playing the master over people, he exposed it. Its power to fool us over what life is comes out in his parable of the rich fool who lived without God. 'Tonight your soul will be required of you. What profit then will your riches be?' 'How is a man to profit if he should win the whole world and lose his soul'

Profit? Jesus warns us that if we live only by the profit motive we've not started to get our accounts right for eternity. The only way we can balance our books before God is to come as spiritual beggars, poor in spirit, a debtor to his mercy, and ask God to save our life.

And in a daring contrast, the Apostle Peter reminds us money is not our Saviour. 'For we are redeemed not with corruptible things such as silver and gold, but with the precious blood of Christ.'

34

Our Educational Heritage

Many of us owe a real debt to teachers in the classroom.
But where are the theorists taking us? Nothing marks our
generation more than recurring controversy over what and
how to teach in the classroom. The debate was given an
unexpected boost when Prince Charles entered the fray.

The Prince of Wales talked about 'cultural disinheritance'
in the 'land of Shakespeare'. I'd like to talk about our
education heritage in Wales, 'the land of the Bible'.

For example, if you walk along the promenade outside
University College Aberystwyth, you'll see a statue of
T. C. Edwards, Aberystwyth's first principal. In his hand
is a Bible, for him the source of true truth. How did 'Aber'
itself begin? Largely through the myriad pennies taken up
in Sunday School Bible studies throughout Wales. Those
Bible schools launched popular education. They helped
people grasp what God says life is all about. Times change,
but today's crisis in education still lies there—what is life all
about? What are we to believe is true? What are children to
take as right and wrong—is there such a thing? Is my life just
mine? Or will we have to give account of our lives to God?

Biblical disinheritance cuts us off from answers to those
questions. Today's fashion is—what's newest is truest. This
fad for the new has led to Innovation Fatigue: tired out
teachers find the latest is no truer than the last. By contrast,
our biblical inheritance tells us of lasting truth. Truth is

reality as God knows it and he's shown us enough of it to establish what I call the three 'R's of education for life.

First, Reverence—reverence for God. The 'fear of the Lord is the beginning of wisdom.' Without that wisdom, reverence for life, respect for the individual and discipline is a problem. Without it, what do you say to a child five seconds after he says, 'Why not?'

The second of the three 'R's is Revelation. God has told us what is true—Ten Commandments included, (which aren't all that irrelevant to the 'why not?' questions). The great personal discovery of life is to find his truth. Others have found it before you, but it's as new and true for you as it was for them. That gives you continuity with the past and stimulus for today. There's no generation gap conflict in homes where that works. Education prospers.

The third follows—Righteousness or right living as God directs us. Those three 'R's hang together. They give the discrimination to choose between right and wrong, truth and error. Without that, education's aim to foster personal excellence is unattained.

In a schools broadcast called 'Man in the Animal World', the narrator asked children to look at a painting: 'What's that animal you see on the left? Yes, a lion. And in the other corner? An elephant. Behind it? A wolf: all members of the animal kingdom. Do you see any other animals? What about the two by the tree—that's right, the man and the woman—they're animals too. But they are clever, they are the animals with the best brains.'

Well, I suppose we've all grinned at our kids and thought, 'He's a clever little beast isn't he.' But is that all they are—body and brain? A theory that reduces us to that is the worst disinheritance. We lose ourselves, values get 'debunked', and some teachers at least see the jungle creeping closer to the classroom.

35

The Lord is my Shepherd

Psalm 23 applies to so many human situations that there are at least seventy paraphrases of it.

But there's one that's dreadfully different:

> King Cocaine is my shepherd, I shall always want.
> He makes me to lie down in the gutters
> He leads me beside troubled waters
> He destroys my soul
> He drives me into the valley of the shadow of death
> Where I experience great evil.

A recent television film on addiction showed cocaine do just that to a family—a chilling reminder that we can commit ourselves to the power of evil and fall into danger of many kinds.

But the twenty-third psalm speaks of help amidst danger; of a Shepherd who stays with us, when evil is against us. We can know God personally: 'The Lord, my Shepherd'. It's as if God is saying, 'You've got an emergency number for Fire, Police, Ambulance. Well, give me a call before the day of trouble.' Someone once entitled this psalm: 'Dial mine, mine, mine.' That is what the Psalmist had done: he had made the Lord his. So can we. Unless we do, there are so many choices in life that drive us into the valley of the shadow with no help at hand. King Cocaine certainly does. He's no shepherd. He's a wolf, and so is every evil.

One day we all have to go through the valley of the shadow. Jesus, the Good Shepherd, talks of death itself as a wolf. But he fought and overcame it in his resurrection and destroyed its power over anyone who trusts in his victory.

Like the young shepherd who two ministers met on a walking holiday in Snowdonia. For a while the three of them talked about Psalm 23. Taking the boy's left hand they taught him to link each of the first five words — 'The Lord is my Shepherd' — with each of his five fingers. With those five words the shepherd grasped the essence of personal faith.

The following year the men returned for another holiday and went climbing to find their friend. Dusk came and they had no success. On the way back down the mountain they called at a cottage. There on the mantelpiece was the lad's photo. He had died in a storm the previous winter. He was found with his right hand clutching the third finger of his left hand. At the moment of death he was saying: 'The Lord is my Shepherd.' As he went through the valley of the shadow, he had been showing his trust in the Lord: 'I will fear no evil, for you are with me.' In life's greatest emergency there was no call box, no rescue helicopter. But he dialled mine, mine, mine. When the wolf struck, what a reassurance to know the voice of the Good Shepherd:

'I give them eternal life and they shall never perish. Nothing can pluck them out of my hand.'

———

Shepherds are often out on the hills at night. The sheep may be lying down in green pastures or by a quiet stream and all is well. But the Shepherd always needs to be awake for they can be in danger in the shadowy hours of darkness.

> The Lord is my shepherd,
>   I shall lack nothing
> He makes me lie down in green pastures,
> He leads me beside quiet waters
> He restores my soul.
> Even though I walk through the valley of
>   the shadow of death, I will fear no evil,
>   For You are with me.

I once heard a Scottish shepherd tell this story. One moonlit night, at 3.30 am, he was up on the hills with binoculars. Foxes had been troubling the flock. Suddenly, below him he saw a fox working a flock of sheep the way his own dog did. The ewes were in a panic, because the fox was driving their lambs to a boggy place, trying to get the lambs stuck down there, driving them into the valley of death.

Eventually, the shepherd, watching up on the hill in the dark, did one simple thing. He whistled. The fox was off like a shot. The point to grasp is this. The shepherd's eye was on the sheep all the time, even at their most frantic moments, though the panicking sheep did not know this. And when he chose to do so, he drove off the fox.

God does not doze off or sleep. He sees and knows his flock and has ways of rescuing us. Sometimes, when we are least aware of his presence he uses the most unlikely means.

He did so, in January 1943, for Mrs Dulles, sister in law of the American politician. She was living in German occupied France. Her young son Billy was ill with pneumonia. One night a German patrol entered her villa and forced them to dress. They were taken in a lorry towards the mountains. It was a clear night. The sky twinkled with a myriad stars. The lorry stopped, mother and son were ordered out, marched through the snow until the heavy child slid to the ground, his mother unable to carry him any longer. Feeling dreadfully alone and in peril, she prayed.

The patrol lined up and loaded their rifles.

'Haven't you any children of your own? I beg you, free the boy, he is a mere child.' The officer's eyes were cold. He did not respond, but turned towards his patrol.

Billy's head protruded from his blanket as he said:

'Mother, look up at the lovely stars. God is not asleep yet. He is watching us.'

After long seconds of silence the officer's voice barked out, dismissing the soldiers. He turned to Mrs Dulles:

'Yes, I too have children. You are free.'

The lorry drove away and mother and child were left to struggle home through the snow.

A young boy looked up and saw the eye of the Lord in the starry heavens. The improbable means by which

God answered a mother's prayer. Put it another way: The Shepherd up on the hill, who watches his sheep in distress, had acted to see off the fox.

———————

Shepherds keep watch over their flocks by night as well as by day. They have to be both tender and strong as they care for the sheep. The twenty-third Psalm reminds us the Lord is both tender: 'He restores my soul', and firm: 'he leads me in paths of righteousness'.

One night I awoke to a very bright moonlight. Every detail of our garden was lit up by an eerie light. A shooting star flashed across the sky. A distant cock crowed several times over. I had read that the cock crows about 3:30 a.m. I checked the time. Yes, it was 3:35 a.m. I thought of Simon Peter denying his Lord as the cock crowed and weeping bitter tears in the night. But the risen Jesus, the Good Shepherd, had sought Peter out and forgiven him. He did what Psalm 23 promises—he restored his soul and led him back into paths of righteousness. The Lord had done the same thing for David, the writer of Psalm 23, after his deep repentance over his adultery with Bathsheba and the murder of her husband. As these thoughts flashed through my mind, I thought of my 'unseen Shepherd up there on the Hill.' I opened my Bible. I read from the psalms—'Let not my heart be drawn to any evil.'

Some weeks before, I had seen how easily evil does draw people. I was staying away from home, though in a residential area I knew very well, and I'd been forced to work into the early hours of the morning. Before going to bed I looked out into the street. It was again a moonlit night and I saw a woman take a man into her home and into the bedroom opposite. It was not her husband. I saw the whole affair. It was like walking into a room and seeing a video you'd never intended to see. I found myself indignant.

That couple have no idea what I saw. They don't even know that I exist. No doubt, for them, God doesn't exist either. I felt a bit like the unseen shepherd on the hill who watches his flock in the dark, though they don't know he is there. I thought of how Jesus dealt with people who had been drawn into sexual sin. His aim was to restore their soul and lead them back into paths of right living. He would have been firm but tender too. Somehow I found my anger and condemnation giving way to prayer.

Remember what he said when he was asked to condemn a woman caught in the act? 'If any of you is without sin let him cast the first stone.' He did not condone her act, but neither did he reject her. 'Neither do I condemn you. Go, leave your life of sin.' He received her and led her back to a new and changed life. It was the same with the Samaritan woman he met at the well. The current man in her life was number six, though she had no idea Jesus knew that, until he made it plain that he did. 'You'll never find satisfaction that way. You need a new spring of satisfaction within you — the spring of eternal life, which I alone can give you.'

She believed him. When the neighbours in her street, some no doubt deeply offended by her life style, saw the change he made to her life, do you know what they said?

'Now we know that this man really is the Saviour of the world.'

Life can seem empty in the 'small hours'. Psalm 23 can give comfort for the night and strength for the morrow.

In these days of tubeless tyres we tend to forget about the old inner rubber tubes. You could patch the odd puncture, but eventually they'd perish, and nothing could save them. When Psalm 23 says, 'He restores my soul,' it's that threatening word 'perish' it has in mind. Without God, human life is perishing. We can try patching it up, but the fabric's gone — we, ourselves, need to be restored. Drive on a motorway with a perished tyre and there's a blow out. Life has its blow outs too. So it is the most remarkable good news possible that he restores me with a life the Bible calls imperishable. The Anglican Prayer Book renders it 'he converts my soul', that is, we can exchange our old perishable life for his new life.

There's a story of a BBC radio star of the fifties that shows us how. Many of you will remember the radio serial called Paul Temple. Spine-chilling in those days. Its splendid theme music was called Coronation Scot. The man who recorded that music for the BBC was a top dance band leader. He broadcast regularly and gave dancing lessons over the air and many well known names were linked to his programme. Yet, in spite of success and money, things began to go badly wrong. He was unhappy. His marriage and professional life were falling apart. One night, sleeping tablets in his pocket, he decided to take his own life.

While he was waiting at St John's Wood Underground station, a group of young people came on to the platform singing. To his amazement he realized they were not drunk, they were singing a hymn. One of them got talking to him about Christ. As sometimes happens, God met this man when his old life was at the point of blow out. Half an hour later, in the quietness of St Martin-in-the-Fields he turned to God for forgiveness. The man who had begun the day thinking the whole fabric of his life was perishing found Christ gave him a new start. God restored his soul with inward, imperishable life.

He describes the renewing power of God like this:

'I surrendered my life to Christ. I knew that he had been to the cross and died for me. My life was completely changed. Old things passed away, all things had become new.'

From then on he used his talents in the service of Christ.

Its a personal example of what this psalm is all about. The Shepherd seeks, finds, retrieves, and revives us. Why? To lead us through this life into his presence. The word 'perish' cannot coexist in his company.

'Goodness and mercy shall follow me all the days of my life, and I will dwell in the house of the Lord for ever.'

36

A City of Refuge

Reading the Old Testament is sometimes like watching television news. We follow the camera into refugee camps in the desert. We see people fleeing cities, with nowhere to go. But Biblical reporters have an extra dimension of the prophet. They see the way through life's deserts and troubles to the eternal city of God. Psalm 107 is an example:

> Some wandered in desert wastelands,
>   finding no way to a city
>   where they could settle.
> They were hungry and thirsty
>   and their lives ebbed away.
> Then they cried out to the Lord
>   in their trouble
> and he delivered them
>   from their distress.
> He led them by a straight way
>   to a city where they could settle.
>
> Ps. 107: 4–7

People's need of rescue doesn't change, either in deserts or modern cities. The psalm's 'word pictures' fit anywhere—lost, hungry, homeless people. These pictures depict painful facts—life's emergencies constantly calling for emergency aid. They are also metaphors that point to real spiritual lostness, and they point the way out of it to God. For our need of eternal rescue doesn't change either. The Bible's most urgent questions relate to settling our eternal destiny. The psalm tells how God guides us to a secure city. The Bible's full, big picture emphasises how tangible and real heaven is. It's the place to go to from here.

You may remember the programme 'In Town Tonight'. It opened with the roar of London's traffic. And then a great shout, STOP. Traffic was stilled and the programme interviewed visitors to the city. 'Why are you here in town tonight? Are you just passing through? Where do you go on to from here?'

It's good to stop a moment before we hit the traffic roar. Where are we heading? Just into town? OK. We know our way into town. But we can also know Christ as the way to God. He brings us to a city to settle in for ever. The heavenly city is a picture of God's permanent gift of eternal life in Christ.

The Bible won't allow us to settle for this life only. Here nothing lasts. Permanent building societies don't provide the permanent city. And the deepest decay lies, not in buildings, but in the lives of people. Structurally, the fittest of us are less permanent than some of the places we live in. They'll stand after we've gone. We are passing through... but to where? The modern concrete jungle hardly beckons us to heaven.

But in Christ there is permanent good news for us and for the city. God doesn't give up on its citizens. In what is still the world's great problem city, Christ died for the world's sinners—to bring us to God and to make us citizens of heaven. As the Risen Lord, he calls all who will follow him to the city with eternal foundations, whose builder is God. The psalm sees the redeemed of the Lord pouring into it, spanning the east-west, north-south divides, travelling from every nation under heaven, brought into harmony by the Saviour of the world.

So, let's not forget our true citizenship or where we really belong. The coming of the eternal city of God will certainly bring future divine rescue and justice. But we are also to represent that here and now. To seek right relationships with men and with God in the thick of city life. To show the love of Christ that can bring rescue even to those whose lives are a ruin of what they were created to be.

My Chains Fell Off

My three-year-old son once said to me as he watched me go through the gate of the prison I was visiting, 'Daddy, if I'm a good boy, can I go to prison with you next time?' How we laughed. It's not good boys who go to prison. It affronts us to see good guys in prison. How elated we've been to see hostages freed. But how free are any of us really? Good guys included—those who have never been near prison. When the advent hymn says, 'Christ comes the prisoners to release, to free the captive mind,' it includes everyone. The chains Psalm 107 describes are not confined to those in jail.

> Some sat in darkness
>   and the deepest gloom,
>   prisoners suffering in iron chains,
>   for they rebelled against
>   the words of God
>   and despised the counsel
>   of the most High.
> So he subjected them to bitter labour.
>   They stumbled and there was
>   none to help.
> Then they cried unto the LORD
>   in their trouble
>   He delivered them from their distress.
> He brought them out of darkness
>   and the deepest gloom
>   and broke away their chains.
>
>   Ps. 107: 10–14

Sometime or other we get the feeling we are our own prison. Locked into inner failure or uncertainty. Unable to walk away from the guy we really are. It was not meant to be so. God's word provides a window on ourselves. We aren't prisoners without light. We were created to know him and enjoy both this sparkling world and eternity. Free to love and serve him and others, to be so free from selfish concerns we would want to live for others, finding our fulfilment in making them as full of constant joy as we are.

But that's not how it is with us. Even the good we want to do we often fail to do, the evil we would reject we often commit. It chains the good guy too. 'Gentlemen', says Anthony Burgess, expounding C. S. Lewis, 'Gentlemen can relish evil while professing a devotion to the good.' 'Who can set me free?' asks Paul, that Pharisaic gentleman. Thank God there is a way out, through Jesus Christ our Lord.

Being set free in Christ is a different thing from improving our lot in life. That would be to confuse better prison conditions with getting out of prison. When Terry Waite was a hostage he was chained to a wall and had no window. Ian Richter was able to have daily runs, but it was prison for both. The answer was not amelioration of their conditions, welcome as they were. The only answer was freedom. They wanted back what they'd lost.

Jesus gives us back the freedom we've lost. He breaks the chains of past guilt, present sin and future death. He opens the door to eternal life and the enthralling capacity to enjoy God. Don't miss it. Without it, all other improvements still leave us in prison, facing death, the unscaleable prison wall. With unique authority Jesus calls us to cross over into life.

So, the real freedom issue is this—are we just looking for more freedoms within the confines of this world? Or will we seek the truth that sets us free to love God and each other? The psalmist describes how dogged unbelief blinds us to these things. But he also anticipates the change that comes when Jesus, the light of the world, dispels darkness and shows the way out. Charles Wesley's words reflect much of Psalm 107:

> Long my imprisoned spirit lay,
> Fast bound in sin and nature's night.
> Thine eye diffused a quickening ray,
> I woke, the dungeon flamed with light.
> My chains fell off, my heart was free
> I rose went forth and followed thee.

Preventive Medicine

Preventive medicine is gaining ground. Some illnesses we can learn to avoid. Wise eating: less artery blockage; no smoking: fewer chest troubles; one partner: little chance of sexual disease. The sickness described in Psalm 107 is the preventable kind, the kind we bring on ourselves when we persist in pleasures we know will harm us. 'What a fool I've been, if only I'd listened,' we sometimes hear from the drug victim.

Some were sick through their
   sinful ways,
 and because of their iniquities
   suffered affliction.
They loathed any kind of food,
 and they drew near to the gates of death.
Then they cried to the Lord
   in their trouble
and he delivered them
   from their distress;
He sent forth his word and healed them,
 and delivered them from destruction.

Ps. 107: 17–20

During one of Jesus' healing miracles he roundly rejected the suggestion of some bystanders that the man's own or his parents' sin must have caused his illness. He made it abundantly clear that for one human to blame another for being ill is not on.

But there is a difference between self-righteous condemnation and wise warnings against harming ourselves. On another occasion, Jesus healed a man whose illness could have been prevented had he lived wisely. So, he warned against repeating the folly. 'Look,' said Jesus when he gave him a check up later, 'Don't go on sinning or something worse may happen.'

Those are startling words. But they come from the most compassionate of all healers. They are wise counsel and command, from someone who knows the issues of life and death. They are a vital warning for our generation. It's perfectly clear Jesus saw sleeping around as wrong. He warns that unless we hear that for ourselves, things can go wrong. It's not a religious nag. It's preventive medicine to protect the innocent, a protective fence built for our good.

By common consent people have drifted from firm convictions about right and wrong. We think moral commands are restrictions rather than protections. This acceptance that anything goes has victims as well as participants. AIDS sufferers can be both. When we've been taught for so long it is our right to take the quickest route to short term pleasure, we get hooked on pleasure as the goal in life. Therefore preventing any disease that can come via pleasure is a problem. We rarely think a medical statistic will include me. Statistics about risk, without a moral conviction that sleeping around is wrong, give poor protection.

The psalm gives God's means of bringing change in us. 'He sent forth his word and healed them.' His word is a Health and Life Manual in this area as in others. In it, God our Maker gives directives about quality of life. If you seek sexual joy says God, the creator of sexuality, you'll not find it by just going for it. The norm for deepening it is one partnership for life. And lots of couples can tell you how God's love has constantly renewed their own. Some local sixth formers were astonished when told making good lovers and experiencing sexual joy is a very biblical thing. When Jesus tells us to confine those joys to marriage, he's protecting us from harming them and ourselves. Prevention has always been better than cure.

Our Littleness

Nothing reminds us of our littleness like the sea. In face of the storm we face our insignificance. The hurricane shakes us into seeing that in a world of gigantic forces, we live not only by good management, but by permission of wind and wave, and our eternal Father, strong to save. This parable from Psalm 107 speaks of the rescue of sailors, at their wits end in the storm. But the voyage of life itself is here too.

> Others went down to the sea in ships,
>   doing business on the great waters.
> They saw the works of the Lord,
>   his wonderful deeds in the deep.
> For he spoke and stirred up the tempest
>   that lifted high the waves.
> They mounted up to the heavens
>   and went down to the depths.
> In their peril their courage melted away.
>   They reeled and staggered
>   like drunken men,
>   they were at their wits end.
> Then they cried out to the Lord
>   in their trouble
>   and he brought them
>   out of their distress.
> He guided them to their desired haven

Ps. 107: 23–8; 30b

Perhaps you recall that incident in the Bible when Jesus was asleep in a fishing smack and a fierce storm whipped up the sea. They almost went down. 'Lord, save us,' they cried. He got up, stilled the waves, and there was a great calm. 'Who is this that even the winds and waves obey Him?' they asked. Christ, though he is true man, is not confined to our littleness. He became man, but he is also God, the Creator. The disciples eventually knew for sure who he was, for even the hurricane of death did not destroy him. He came through it into resurrection, as he said he would.

But when Jesus demonstrated his claim to be God during the course of his ministry many rejected it utterly. 'Who do you think you are?' they said in a tone of dismissal. But how majestic is the true answer to that question. Jesus knew he was the eternal Son of God. He had come to seek the lost and to save us from the ultimate storm of eternal judgment. To believe that is a mark of the Christian disciple. Without him we're lost in a sea of troubles.

This passage from Psalm 107 turns my mind to the many convinced Christian men who have been sailors, like Captain John Brown, Commodore of the Union Castle Line. At a retirement celebration in 1950, he told a gathering of 3000 people: 'When as a young officer of twenty-five I came to Christ as a guilty, trembling sinner, he freely forgave all and I found his promise true, "He that comes to me I will never cast out." Since then I have frequently looked death in the face, sunk three times, twice by torpedoing, bombed on several occasions. Always, however, I have found him with me. I have had the joy of preaching Christ to thousands of troops and passengers who have sailed with me, several of whom have come to know Christ as their own personal Saviour.'

One example was a man who was making shipwreck of his life. He had embezzled his insurance company, deserted his wife and family, and signed on in a Union Castle liner. One night he was swept over board. None discovered it for twenty minutes. Brown ordered the ship to turn, praying fervently for the man's safety. After an hour cries were heard over the port side. He was pulled aboard with a leg torn by a shark. The story was flashed to newspapers across the world, and of course, the truth about his embezzlement came out. The captain gathered fellow Christians in the crew together to pray that the man would find Christ as Saviour and return home a new man. The greatest joy to the captain came when he was not only reunited with his family, his debts paid, but when he repented of sin and went home a saved man, in more senses than one.

37

Revival Hymns

Isaac Watts—'Joy to the World'

We are all used to arguments about worship. Some family will come home from church on Sunday and one of the teenagers will say, 'Wasn't the singing boring. Can't we have something more lively?' When twenty-year-old Isaac Watts and his father came home from church one morning, the young student complained strongly against the dreary way the Psalm paraphrases had been droned out, line by line. There were few hymns at all in England in those days and psalm singing was in the doldrums. 'Give us something better Isaac,' retorted his father.

By the next Sunday, Watts had his first hymn ready. When his *Hymns and Spiritual Songs* appeared in 1707, the year Charles Wesley was born, a revolution in congregational worship was under way. Watts' voice still moves the nation. Who, even today, in a land that no longer knows its psalms, does not respond to 'O God, our help in ages past'? Watts' rendering of Psalm 90 is a national event, especially at times of remembrance. And when Christians worldwide gather to remember the death of Christ, 'When I survey the wondrous cross on which the Prince of glory died' are the words that rise so often in our hearts.

The sheer cheerfulness of Watts uplifts us too: 'Religion never was designed to make our pleasures less,' sings this profoundly God honouring Calvinist:

> Come, we that love the Lord,
> And let our joys be known.

Of course, his joy comes from believing what God says. Heaven is a land of pure delight, God is the spring of all his joys. This in spite of the nail-biting frustrations of a fallen world where 'time bears all its sons away.' When, as a leading astronomer in his day, Watts scanned the whole realm of nature, he did not look out at a meaningless universe. 'Ere the blue heavens were stretched abroad from everlasting was the Word.' It is God, our mighty maker, who 'built the earth, spread the sky, fixed the starry lights on high.' He is also the one who 'sent his Son with power to save, from guilt and darkness and the grave.'

His grasp of the cosmic scope to salvation has a message for our polluted planet. We don't live on a random orb in space at risk from our own excesses. The whole realm of nature is not mine or yours. It belongs to the Prince of glory. Therefore joy is not just for me and you. There is a message of hope and 'Joy to the earth!' Why? 'The Saviour reigns!'

Could I suggest that in this exuberant rendering of Psalm 98 Watts conveys the Bible's perspective on our planet's future? It calls upon the earth and every human heart to receive her King and prepare room for him; let men and nature, fields and flocks, hills and plains repeat the sounding joy—the Saviour reigns. Only when his righteousness rules will earth's creeping curse be removed and a green earth be secured. While the human tenant is in revolt, he continues to abuse his Master's property. So, says Watts, in words set to the joyous tune of his great contemporary, Handel:

> No more let sins and sorrows grow,
> Nor thorns infest the ground;
> He comes to make His blessings flow
> Far as the curse is found.

Charles Wesley—'And Can it be?'

On October 4, 1738, Watts, by then a famous figure in the nation, had two visitors—John and Charles Wesley. The brothers had hardly begun their great work, for they had only recently come to salvation in Christ. All we know about the visit is a tantalizing note in Wesley's diary:

'1.30 at Dr Watts. Conversed. 2.30 Walked, singing.'

That's all. But what a picture to imagine. Watts and the Wesleys in three part harmony, singing each others hymns. Which ones, we wonder? Perhaps that great hymn of Dr Watts, which we know was upon John Wesley's lips when he died, 'I'll praise my Maker while I have breath, and when my voice is lost in death.'

Not surprisingly, the Wesley brothers had sang together at the beginning of their Christian lives. Charles had found peace three days before John and he immediately wrote a hymn. They sang it with great joy on the night a troop of friends brought John to Charles in triumph, declaring, 'I believe.'

That spiritual birthday hymn is a manifesto, longing to reach the unreached masses for Christ:

> Outcasts of men, to you I call,
> Harlots and publicans and thieves
> Christ spreads his arms to embrace you all;
> Sinners alone His grace receive.
> Come O my guilty brethren, come.

And how they came! Quite soon John tells of winning ten prisoners in dreadful Newgate prison. He spent the night in the cells and went with them in the cart to the place of execution. 'It was one of the most triumphant hours I have ever known,' he wrote.

Such triumphs of grace were to stretch across another fifty incredible years as they preached and sang their way into the hearts of a nation.

Wesley's hymns teach us more than all the histories ever written about God's truth and power which 'brought men—degraded and brutalized beyond description—to listen to John Wesley as to a prophet of God, and to Whitefield as to an angel from heaven.'

They didn't just listen—to get them to do that was wonder enough. Multitudes were converted. We see and feel for ourselves the wonder of it as the hymn writer saw God's Spirit at work before his eyes among the thousands who gathered in field and street:

> He speaks and listening to His voice,
> New life the dead receive
> The mournful, broken hearts rejoice,
> The humble poor believe.
> He breaks the power of cancelled sin
> He sets the prisoner free.

What is the power that freed imprisoned men, men fast bound in chains of sin? Wesley never stops telling us. He is always at Calvary, the place of God's amazing love:

> And can it be that I should gain
> An interest in the Saviour's blood
> Died he for me who caused his pain?
> For me who him to death pursued?

His constant theme is the stupendous mystery that the Immortal dies and bled for Adam's helpless race. 'How can it be, that Thou, my God, shouldst die for me?'

John Newton—'Amazing Grace'

> Amazing grace! How sweet the sound,
> That saved a wretch like me.
> I once was lost, but now am found,
> Was blind but now I see.

John Newton's hymn 'Amazing Grace' climbed to the top of the charts in our non church-going age. When Newton was born in 1725, the churches of Britain were also in rapid decline—Watts bemoans it in one of his hymns. Within the churches Watts inspired new heights of praise in worship. But that did not stop the decline in numbers. The tide turned through revival and preaching. Complete outsiders like Newton began to turn to Christ, though his experience reminds us that it was God's amazing grace that wrought the change in the nation, not crowd psychology—for Newton was saved alone and met no other Christian for six years.

Newton called himself an infidel and libertine. His life reflected the times—street violence, gang muggings, drunken police, a gin craze as bad as our drug threat. Today's soccer violence pales before the brutality of eighteenth century sport, juicily spiced with bare fist fighting between women. Britain's reputation was at rock bottom. Our main revenues came from drink traffic and slave trade.

Out of that slave trade, grace 'saved a wretch like me,' says Newton. The man who later sings in Amazing Grace, 'through many dangers, toils and snares, I have already come' is putting it mildly.

After remarkable deliverances in storm, shipwreck and raging fever he was awed to seek after God while at sea. He was deeply affected by the story of the prodigal son. He sighed with relief when he read, 'He is able to save to the uttermost,' and for six solitary years his faith grew in adversity. Then he met another Christian captain in port. 'We spent every evening together. I was all ear, his teaching warmed my heart...my conceptions became more evangelical...I began to expect to be preserved by the mighty power and promise of God through faith in an unchangeable Saviour.'

One of his hymns shows the robust confidence he learned on board:

> Begone unbelief, my Saviour is near,
> With Christ in the vessel, I smile at the storm.

He became a dynamic and forthright preacher in London, his hymns showing the complete revolution in his life:

> Fading is the worldling's pleasure,
> All his boasted pomp and show,
> Solid joys and lasting treasure,
> None but Zion's children know.

There was also a tenderness in him too. Congregations still sense it:

> How sweet the name of Jesus sounds,
> in a believers ear.
> It soothes his sorrows, heals his wounds
> and drives away his fear.

It is a sweet irony of amazing grace that Newton, the ex-slave ship captain was used in the conversion of William Wilberforce. Newton preached a famous series of sermons on the biblical texts of Handel's *Messiah*, which was reaching the crowds like a modern musical. After one of the sermons Wilberforce came to Newton, 'affected' he says ' by a sense of my great sinfulness.' 'When I came away I found my mind in a calm and tranquil state.' The grace that won a slave trader, led eventually to the freeing of the slaves. Has there ever been a clearer example of the social impact of evangelical conversion?

William Williams — 'Guide me O Thou Great Jehovah'

And now to Wales and the revival hymns of William Williams, Pantycelyn. We have seen how Charles Wesley met Watts soon after he became a Christian. Williams Pantycelyn came to Christ in that same year. Through this trio, the hymn attained its finest hour as a servant of evangelical truth. Watts had laid the foundations. He knew that human imagination must not take a higher place than the truths of Scripture. He patiently persuaded his fellow Calvinists that hymns could portray the wonder of our close personal relationship with Christ without losing the transcendence of God's revealed truth.

Pantycelyn also knew that. If he was to convey true love for Christ in his hymns, he must become steeped in the poetry and content of the Bible. No poet, he says, could serve God without knowing the beauty of his art and the source of his knowledge lay there. Where will you find the imagery, the powerful turns of phrase, the daring comparisons, stirring and strange thoughts, more than in the Psalms, the Song of Solomon, Job, the prophets, and Revelation? Pantycelyn, says Professor Bobi Jones, is both moved by an all consuming feeling, and displays impressive intellectual powers subject to the discipline of the scriptures

Derec Llwyd Morgan shows how this sensitive poetic discipline ensured something vital. It meant the spiritual experiences Christians sang about, reflected the truths of the Bible. The hymns helped bring the Bible to life in the singer's soul and gave them bread from heaven to live day by day. This biblical nourishment made holding on to Christ a pleasure both to the senses and to the intellect. The pilgrim in this barren land who suffers troubles on his journey home to the Father's house is not on a flight of fancy. Hymns with this idiom are rooted in the power of the gospel of Christ to bring sinners home, through the wilderness, to glory.

The A40 road between Brecon and Llandovery winds its way through some lonely mountains. A sharp turn and rise in the road takes you quickly past a little sign post to Pentre Ty Gwyn, easily missed. I happen to know it, because down that road lies the farm where my mother was born. But down that same road is another farm called Pantycelyn, its visitors book filled with illustrious names like David Lloyd-George and others from countries far and wide. There, over two hundred years ago, Williams Pantycelyn died. The farm looks towards the barren Cambrian mountains:

> Guide me, Oh Thou great Jehovah,
> Pilgrim through this barren land
> I am weak but Thou art mighty
> Hold me with they powerful hand.

Williams had been too weak to leave his room for the last months of his life. 'Think what a disappointment it must be to a man like me, who has travelled nearly three thousand miles every year for over fifty years, now able to move less than forty feet in a day, from the fireside to the bed. This is how God wishes to deal with me, and it is well.'

'It is well'. In his final trial Williams was practising what he had preached in his hymns. The pilgrim was looking ahead to glory:

> When I tread the verge of Jordan,
> bid my anxious fears subside…
> Songs of praises I will ever give to thee.

During more than fifty years, songs of praise had poured from him as he roved and ranged among the rough mountains and wild precipices of Wales, searching for anyone to whom he could commend the love of Christ. In all he covered 111,800 miles. No wonder he prays, 'May the fiery, cloudy pillar lead me all my journey through'.

This idiom of the pilgrim on his journey home to the Father's house runs right through the hymn. Christ gives us bread from heaven to live on day by day. He is our Strong deliverer, our strength and shield. His powerful hand holds us steady when the journey gets tougher. This was not just a poetic image for Williams. Its truth enabled him to say, 'It is well,' in the face of death. Its comfort derives from the Bible's message of the real power of the gospel of Christ to bring sinners home, through the wilderness, to glory:

> Death of death and hell's destruction
> land me safe on Canaan's side.

When the hymn was printed in America that last line appeared as 'Land my safe on Canaan's side.' 'No you can't take it with you brother,' commented the amused discoverer of the misprint. But take the real message of this hymn to heart, and it will take us to heaven. The warm strength of Cwm Rhondda, its world famous tune, helps lift our hearts heavenwards.

In Eden

William Williams began his Christian life in Talgarth, a village lying in the shadow of the Brecon Beacons. When he visited there as a young medical student of twenty, Williams shared the cold indifference of his contemporaries to the Christian faith. Some church historians have called it 'the Glacial Epoch'. But things were starting to change. Within a few decades, the whole life of our nation altered under the influence of the Methodist Revival. Williams' hymns were themselves to be one of the powerful means of this change.

But Williams had no inkling of such things the day he stopped to join a crowd listening to a sermon preached in Talgarth churchyard. The young preacher—Hywel Harris—had himself not long been converted to Christ. The influence he was to have in Wales is comparable to that of John Wesley in England. If you ever holiday in the Brecon Beacons National Park, wander into Talgarth church. You will find on the wall a thrilling tribute to Harris' extraordinary ministry.

His sermon had a life-changing effect on Williams. 'It was the day I first heard heaven's summons,' he tells us. In that same remarkable year, Charles Wesley came to his assurance of salvation. Williams and Wesley are spiritual poets of similar stature. Their hymns share the same Christ-centred themes and have had the same life changing impact on people.

England and Wales sang in harmony in those revival hymns. The theme that recurs most is the cross of Christ. They sang of it abundantly and gratefully. And no wonder:

Faith, see the place, and see the tree
Where heaven's Prince, instead of me,
Was nailed to bear my shame.

In Eden, sad indeed that day
My countless blessings fled away,
My crown fell in disgrace.
But on victorious Calvary
That crown was won again for me—
My life shall all be praise!

Many a critic finds the language of blood morbid, says Morgan:

> Yes, of course, it is to those who choose to view the passion of the cross unsympathetically, that is, without seeing its victory…The central paradox of the Christian faith is that the sin that sent Christ to his cross was vanquished through the cross. What God's children were doing when they sang was rejoicing in the effect of the blood. Without that, they would have no cause to rejoice, no object on which to pour their love, no entry into heaven. No wonder they sang of it almost without cease.

Jesus, Jesus all-sufficient

If you talked to Williams Pantycelyn about treasure, worth or riches he would talk to you about Jesus. That's where he found those things in abundance:

Jesus, Jesus, all-sufficient
Beyond telling is thy worth
In Thy name lie greater treasures
Than the richest found on earth.

That tells us something of Williams' view of the Lord Jesus. He is always singing about his supremacy. He's incomparable. He's not just superior to others. No one exists to compete with him. He is supreme because he is God. He is 'heaven's delight'. And if he is the delight of heaven, who on earth can surpass him?

In the gracious face there's beauty
Far surpassing everything
Found in all the earth's great wonders
Mortal eye has ever seen.

Williams lived in an exciting age. Many of the world's great wonders were seen for the first time by human eyes through the telescope and microscope. The age of Newton had been one of the most astonishing eras of scientific discovery and the new knowledge was spreading fast. It was a kind of information explosion.

Though so many of these scientists were Christians, most of the spreading of the information was organized by the opponents of Christianity like Rousseau and Voltaire. The best media men of the day didn't like Christian truth. Williams made it his task to counter this and to put Christ where he belonged — as Lord of all. He enthused over every kind of knowledge and popularized it through his long epic poems, such as 'A View of Christ's Kingdom.'

These epics, all written in Welsh of course, were a kind of encyclopedia in which the whole range of culture in this world came under the unifying principle of the Kingdom of Christ. It was Christ who gave life cohesion and fulfilment. He alone enables us to live in harmony with God, with ourselves, with the created world around us, with history and with our destiny.

Christ is the only hero of these poems. He is supreme in them as he is in the hymns. Even while the poet enthuses about the wealth and wonders of the world of nature and science, he fixes his gaze dramatically on the Son of God. There is a beauty about Jesus himself that surpasses all the blessings this life can give:

> He's greater than his blessings,
>   he's greater than his grace,
> Far greater than his actions,
>   whatever you may trace;
> I'll plead for faith, gifts, cleansing,
>   yearn for them and implore,
> But on him only, always,
>   I'll look and lean far more.

Williams of course, wants us to look too. What he longs for, he also wants us to long for:

> Tell me thou art mine O saviour,
> Grant me an assurance clear:
> Banish all my dark misgivings
> Still my doubting, calm my fear.

> O, my soul within me yearneth
> Now to hear thy voice divine
> So shall grief be gone forever
> Despair shall be no longer mine

In the incomparable person of Christ, Williams says, we find supreme fulfilment:

> Beautiful and holy being
> In Thyself is joy divine
> Confident, I seek Thy presence
> Pure happiness is mine.'

Welshmen tend to show their emotions more openly than the English. During the exciting times of the eighteenth century revival there were many reserved English gentlemen, kind and Christian to the core, who were alarmed at some of the enthusiasm of Welsh crowds when singing Pantycelyn's hymns. The Welsh were a bit aggrieved that their more staid English friends accused them of being 'Jumpers, Jumpers' at their meetings. One of the Welsh preachers thought Englishmen, with their reserve were 'Sleepers, Sleepers' who needed waking up in worship. Well, it was only a very minor squabble, and Williams Pantycelyn was the first to see the emptiness of mere mass emotion in meetings.

But he longed that people would share his own deep love of God. In 1762, the widespread spiritual blessing which rolled like a wave across Wales came mainly as a result of his new book of hymns. His younger friend, Thomas Charles, described the power of his hymns to convey the truths he rejoiced in, to the singing crowds:

> [Williams] would frequently mount on very strong wings which would lift him into heights of splendour as he wrote about Christ and his cross. Some verses in his hymns were like coals of fire warming and firing every emotion. People were impelled to sing them over and over again, until they broke into shouting and leaping for joy.

The sight of great multitudes meeting out of doors to hear and sing about Christ was something new, and at first astonished people. They had been more used to other kinds of crowds. Don't forget, this is the age of Hogarth we are talking about. His paintings depict the growth of crowd violence in town and country as the gin craze gathered momentum. 'Drunk for 1d, dead drunk for 2d, free straw' went the invitation. Those kind of gatherings damaged home and families.

At the same time, the revival gathered pace. And the excitements these crowds experienced gradually had a very different effect on the nation's life. Revival joy was elevating and transforming. After all, to be overwhelmed by a sense of God's love is the most glorious experience known to man. It led to holy and responsible living, and in the end saved many from the gin craze as they found something better in life.

Williams Pantycelyn was a wise counsellor to thousands of young men and women who had found that what Christ gives is far better. They sang about it with great emotion: 'All the world's distracting voices, all the enticing tones of ill, at thine accents, mild, melodious are subdued'. But Williams was not only a gifted hymn writer, enabling people to sing about the change Christ had brought to their lives. He also taught many to demonstrate that change by genuine discipleship.

He gave enormous energy to this counselling. For example, he gave guidance on courtship and marriage to countless people. Williams wrote helpfully on this and other concerns of the young people he met regularly. He wrote in a dynamic way, using a kind of novel form. His characters leap into life. The relevance of the bible to their relationships is woven into real life stories. Williams got these stories from the multitudes of young people who shared with him their spiritual needs in the Methodist experience meeting. He wasn't afraid of them leaping for joy as they sang, as long as their spiritual happiness was genuine and issued in lives of goodness and godliness.

38

Harmony

May the God of steadfastness and encouragement grant
you to live in such harmony with one another in accord
with Christ Jesus that together you may with one voice
glorify the God and Father of our Lord Jesus Christ.
Welcome one another, therefore as Christ has welcomed
you, for the glory of God.

Romans 15: 5–7

Our Aim

The story is told of the eastern dignitary who was a guest at
a symphony concert. At the end he asked if he could hear
the first tune again, and so the overture was struck up. But
he shook his head. No, the first one. After some puzzlement
it was realized he meant the 'A' of the oboe and the sound of
the orchestra getting into tune with that. It was back to the
basics of getting into harmony.

What should our common aim as Christians be according
to these scriptures from Romans 15? Getting into harmony
with one another in accord with Christ Jesus. We are
committed to the harmony our own message proclaims. Our
passage makes it clear that the true principle of harmony is
love for Christ's people for Christ's sake.

A symphony orchestra is made up of instruments of
different shapes and sizes and sounds. They are played
in different ways—some scrubbed, some banged, others
blown. What possible harmony would you expect between

a piccolo, bubbling away gaily through life, and a thumping, ponderous big bass drum or a groaning double bass? But harmony between such instruments is not only possible, it is expected. They all join together, which is what harmony basically means. But what a difference when they play not only their own part, but play together. 'With one voice glorify the God and Father of our Lord Jesus Christ' (v. 6).

Our Attitude

How can we get into such harmony? It depends so much on your attitude says Paul. 'We are not to please ourselves; let each of us please his neighbour for his good, to edify him' (vv. 1–2). Before the conductor enters and the concert begins there is a cacophony of noisy sound as these different instruments play away at whatever they please. Supposing some persisted in playing whatever they pleased after the conductor brought them to order and they began to perform. Imagine what would happen if all the bass trombones in an orchestra decided to please themselves, to play as loudly and as long as they pleased, any note they pleased. The audience and the rest of the orchestra may as well go home. Just pleasing myself is never the way to harmony. 'Selfism', the psychiatrists tell us, is the key of the decade. It can't work. Harmony implies variety, rich variety. But it is not the variety of everyone going his own way, demanding his own rights: it is the harmony of each looking to his own duties, his own part to play, and by that means safeguarding each other's rights — the other's good. Marriage partners will know harmony involves cooperation for mutual good. That will involve timing, listening to the other player, knowing how and when to say a thing and how and when not to say a thing. Otherwise two battling 'selves' get locked in power struggles. It leads to the feminist anguish of Simon de Beavoir, that 'marriage is hell.' Simply pleasing myself will always lead to something like that for the other person.

Sheer self pleasing will also mean little or no personal spiritual discipline and little enjoyment of corporate worship. I started to play the viola at school but soon stopped doing regular personal practise and then began skipping orchestra practice. I still remember the day when the music master and I came face to face in a narrow corridor, I having until then succeeded in avoiding him. It was a kind of day of judgement, and I wasn't ready for meeting him, was I? 'Boy, if everyone in school was like you we'd have no orchestra.'

If everyone in the fellowship pleased himself, like you and I are tempted to do sometimes, how much harmony and welcoming of one another would there be? I need a real personal relationship to Christ to realize he has welcomed a sinner like me. I need corporate fellowship with other Christians to adjust to the glorious fact that he also has welcomed forgiven sinners like you—and therefore so should I. 'Welcome one another, therefore, as Christ has welcomed you, to the glory of God.' Nothing should delight us more than to welcome new members to join the band. The whole background of the passage is stressing acceptance of Christians with whom we find areas of secondary disagreement. 'Paul will not dismiss someone with less light because he, Paul, has got more light,' says Robert Haldane.

As always the perfect attitude is seen in the example of Christ. 'For even Christ did not please himself' (v. 3). If Christ had pleased himself in the enjoyment of the rights and privileges that belonged to him, what would have come of our salvation? The path he trod for our salvation involved facing head-on the crashing discord of men's insults and reproach, harsh, jarring, deliberate.

How then can you and I hope to live like Christ? We must find our strength to do so in the constant use of Scripture and in the help of God which accompanies it (vv. 4–5). How do we live in harmony in such a world as this? It's partly a matter of holding the notes God wants you to sing or produce. Our weakness is to slide on to the same note of discord that is being amplified all around us. How can you hold the note when you are being drowned out in a dissonant society? Verses 4–5 give is the key. 'May the God of steadfastness and encouragement grant you steadfastness and encouragement through the Scriptures.'

Harmony Maintained

Which of us can do without encouragement, especially when it comes to maintaining harmony in relationships. The nervous bridegroom, when asked 'Wilt thou have this woman?' replied, 'I wilt.' There is a lot of wilting about. The Greek word for steadfastness is 'holding out'; the Greek word for encouragement is 'holding out joyously'. Verse 5 tells us God himself is the source of these twin graces: to receive them and express them we must come to him. How? The Scripture is the score which we study and whose directions we seek to embody in harmonious living. The living God, the composer of the score, comes to us in and through it in such a personal, inspiring way that we give ourselves, mind, heart, soul and strength, to unite in interpreting what he wants to say to us and through us. We want others to hear and be uplifted, to rejoice and sing with us. The score, that is the Scripture, lives because the great creative Holy Spirit of the Composer himself comes through to us. There is no greater stimulus to personal study of God's word and a corporate listening to that word than to realize that is how God himself gets through—'The Spirit breathes upon the word and gilds the page with light.'

A further point about harmony in the passage is that God is in harmony with himself—he does not contradict himself. 'Whatever was written in former days was written for our learning.' That is the New Testament telling us it is in harmony with the Old Testament. There is an intrinsic harmony between God the author and the Scripture itself, and there is harmony between the two Testaments because he is the author of both. Through his word, God casts new light on all the changing scenes of life and so imparts to our hearts the strength to hold out, and to hold out joyously. How do you get the note of hope from God? By reading it in the scriptural score. How do you hold it out with joy? By having enough breath. Listen to Romans 15: 13. I read it to someone weak and ill in a hospital bed: 'May the God of hope fill you with all joy and peace in believing, so that by the power of the Holy Spirit you may abound in hope.' She said, 'Read it again.' The Holy Spirit put fresh breath, fresh spirit into her. May he put fresh breath into us so we may hold out and hold on, together, joyously, in harmony. This gospel sound is not meant to die away. But you and I have to keep turning to the score and breathing in the Spirit of him who wrote it.

There is a symphony by Haydn, the forty-fifth, which is called the 'Farewell Symphony.' In the last movement each section of the orchestra gets up and leaves, one by one, as the music proceeds, till there is only a solitary violin left and the music finally stops. All over the country today there are Christians like you and me who have heard the joyful sound—Jesus saves. That message shall never die away and Christ shall reign. But let us beware of the fragmentary spirit of the age. Let us not be tempted to walk away from each other, section by section, partly because the discordant note of 'pleasing ourselves' is endemic in the world.

The gospel is not the 'Farewell Symphony', but the Welcome Overture. Come. Come to Christ. Christ welcomes you as you are. So welcome one and all who confess Jesus is Lord and believe in their heart God raised him from the dead. And why? So 'together you may with one voice glorify the God and Father of our Lord Jesus Christ.' George Philip of Glasgow tells how at the close of a symphony concert a famous conductor stilled the applause and said 'I am nothing. The orchestra is nothing. You are nothing. The composer is everything.' Yes, in the great world of life, death and eternity, Christ is everything. Yet he did not please himself, he gave himself for us, he gives his life to us, we who are nothing in ourselves, so he might be everything to us, and together we might find everything in him.

Invitation to Life

39

Incline Your Ear

'Hearken diligently unto me,' says the Lord through Isaiah the prophet, 'Incline your ear and come to me, hear, that your soul may live.'

We can all recall embarrassing moments. One I well remember was in Gatwick Airport, just before a flight to Amsterdam. I had said goodbye to my wife and children at the barrier and gone to look for some friends who I knew would be on the flight.

'Hey,' they said when they saw me, 'they are calling for you on the public address.'

'Who, me?'

'Yes, you. They have called for you twice.'

That made me listen carefully. 'I inclined my ear, I hearkened diligently,' as the Bible passage puts it.

There sure enough it came—would I return to the barrier. When I got there I saw my family waiting, and I soon discovered what was wrong. I was about to fly away with the car keys in my pocket. Somehow I had failed to hear, more than once, an important personal message. It failed to get through to me until my friends called attention to it. Only when they did that, did I really begin to listen.

Preaching the gospel does something like those friends did for me. It aims to call our attention to the fact that God calls to you. He has a personal message you may have missed. When God says, 'Listen, give me your ear. Come to me that your soul may live', he is both giving a command and offering an invitation. The fact it is God's command reminds us it is meant to be obeyed. The fact it is God's invitation assures us there is inexpressible joy if we accept it. This joy usually comes as a great surprise. C. S. Lewis, perhaps the most famous of Christian broadcasters, who died the day President Kennedy was assassinated, described his conversion to Christ as 'Surprised by Joy'. He had for years resented the commands of God. He thought of God as his adversary. But when he knelt in his study and acknowledged that God loved him enough to seek for him, his response was joy, the best possible surprise. I suppose that little telephone advert that says 'Happiness is a warm ear piece' is trying to tell you that a surprise call from someone you love can do you the world of good. What Isaiah tells us is that happiness is a warm heart, a heart surprised that God knows and loves us and personally calls us.

His word in your ear is the warm and glad sound of the gospel. To believe it and receive it is to delight in God's call. That's what Isaiah means when he says, 'Hearken diligently unto me and let your soul delight itself in good things.' Notice the delight in this hymn of Charles Wesley when he described what he had seen in the lives of countless thousands who experienced those good things for themselves:

> Jesus the name that charms our fears
> That bids our sorrows cease.
> 'Tis music in the sinner's ears
> 'Tis life and health and peace.
> He speaks and listening to his voice
> New life the dead receive
> The mournful, broken hearts rejoice
> The humble poor believe.

This message God has for us is about life. 'Tis life, new life, says Wesley in that hymn. 'Hear, that your soul may live,' says our text. Jesus himself put it dramatically and he has every authority to do so—'Truly, truly I say to you, he who believes my word and believes him who sent me has eternal life and does not come into judgement, but has passed from death to life.'

Those words of Jesus sound important. But just as I made my way through that busy airport with my mind on other things and did not hear that important message for me, so we can miss what God has to say. Everyday life can be busy, noisy. Isaiah preached his message in a busy, noisy market place. He calls out, 'Why do you spend your money for that which is not bread and your labour for that which does not satisfy?' Of course, there were plenty of bargains, selling was brisk, business was good, and why not? But Isaiah has perspective. He saw the depths. He saw that all the pursuit of novelties and present sensations left men with irrelevancies and emptiness. He saw deeper. He saw there were evil ways and unrighteous thoughts. He saw a hard world, a cynical world, a sceptical world, a cut and thrust world, an 'I'm alright Jack' world, an 'I want more' world: a world where the righteous man perishes and no one takes it to heart. A violent, indulgent world; rushing about fast, but lost, with nowhere to go. Every ox knows its master, said Isaiah, but the people he yearned over had no idea about their Creator.

It is but a step to our 'Twentieth Century Blues' — 'In this strange confusion, chaos or illusion, people seem to lose their way, nothing left to strive for, love or keep alive for,' observed Noel Coward. But Isaiah saw further still. He saw all that could be changed; instead of the useless briars and thorns, there would grow up the noble myrtle and pine tree. Instead of man's ways and man's thoughts, they needed God's ways and God's thoughts. 'For as the heavens are higher than the earth so are my thoughts higher than your thoughts,' says the Lord. To put it plainly we need a world where true, real, good, holy, kind, warm people prevail. A world of help and care and hope and love. A world where children are safe and adults are pure. A world that needs to hear and obey the God who speaks to the heart. God requires 'a heart in every thought renewed, and full of love divine.'

Isaiah knew God's word would work that in those who, in the midst of their own and others unrighteous thoughts and ways, were nevertheless hungry and thirsty for righteousness. That's why he began his invitation to all about him with the words, 'Ho, every one who is thirsty, come', hearken, give ear to what God has to say. 'Seek the Lord while he may be found, call upon him while he is near.' God's word will accomplish in you what it is sent to do.

Why should we listen to what God has to say? For the simple reason that what he says is true. There is no distortion of truth in what God says. These words of Scripture I have quoted to you are the true record of God's voice. The gospel sound is a hi-fi sound, and by that I mean no words can come to you with higher fidelity to the truth than the word of God. Here's another example: 'It is a faithful saying and worthy of our full acceptance that Christ Jesus came into the world to save sinners.'

Let me show the truth of that verse in the lives of two remarkable men in the history of our nation. There was in Cambridge University a young man of great strength of character and energy of spirit. Hugh Latimer was his name. He was keen and formidable in debate. He was a master of oratory. He had been taught in his youth the art of the long bow and how to shoot, not with the strength of his arm only, but with his whole body. With similar wholeheartedness, he flung himself into all the big issues of the period.

One day, another young man of the same university, Thomas Bilney, came to him and said to him how he had been seeking for God—'hungry for God,' as Isaiah puts it. He told him how he had recently began to read the New Testament and how he had found what he had been seeking in the Lord Jesus Christ. Bilney told how, at his first reading of the New Testament he chanced upon that verse I mentioned. 'It is a faithful saying and worthy of our full acceptance that Christ Jesus came into the world to save sinners.' Bilney tells us:

> That one sentence through God's instruction did so exhilarate my heart, which had been so wounded by the guilt of my sins almost to despair, that immediately I seemed to feel a marvellous comfort and quietness. After that scripture began to be more pleasant to me than the honeycomb.

This experience he went and shared with Latimer, later to be a great gospel preaching bishop and truly heroic figure. Bilney quoted the verse that had brought God's grace to him and it was used in Latimer's life in exactly the same way. Years later, Latimer tells us, 'I learned more by that one conversation than by much reading of many books through many years. I now trusted God's word.' Soon Latimer was making a moving plea to the king that the people should be able to read the scriptures.

You see what these outstanding men found trustworthy — God's word is worthy of out attention too. It is truth worth listening to carefully. But if your family is anything like ours at 10am on a Sunday morning, you may not be able to pay attention carefully. There may be all kinds of interference. But one thing I know. If something comes through that you feel is for you and has the ring of truth about it, you will want to listen properly. One of the most wonderful moments in anyone's life is when you begin to stir with the realization that God is saying to you 'listen hard, 'come to me, hear that your soul may live.'

You listen to what God has to say to you because you realize he has something to give you. That's why he's calling for your attention. And Latimer and Bilney and Wesley and Whitefield and myriads from yesterday and from today are witnesses that he does not call in vain. Jesus once said to his disciples, 'The shepherd calls his own sheep by name and they know his voice.' So, says Jesus, my people 'hear my voice and they follow me and I give them eternal life and they shall never perish.' Saul of Tarsus became a new man when he heard God was calling him. 'The Son of God loved me, and gave himself for me.'

'Who? Me?' I said, when the public address system was calling for me. 'Yes, you.'

Through this book, God may be pleased to call you as he announces his word. 'Come to me and I will make an everlasting covenant with you.' Today if you hear his voice, receive what he offers. He offers a free pardon and with it goes the free gift of everlasting life. That free offer is what God intends us to understand by that lavish imagery of the prophet. 'And you who have no money, come, come buy without money and without cost...Turn to the Lord...for he will abundantly pardon.'

Now about the reaction of the person who thinks this is a cheap way to heaven. He says he cannot understand how God can offer something cheap. And of course, if it was cheap, he would be right. But it is not cheap. There is an infinite difference between something cheap and something God gives freely because someone else has already borne the cost. God gives and he has borne all the cost of this free salvation. There lies the infinite difference. That difference comes out in an experience related by Dr Campbell Morgan, once of Westminster Chapel, London.

He had been preaching in a village chapel amongst the Yorkshire coalfields. Into his vestry after the service one evening there came a man of about forty years old, a miner. Follow what then happened in Morgan's own words:

> I looked at him and said 'What's the matter?'
> He replied bluntly, 'I am in hell.'
> I said, 'Why don't you come out?'
> He replied, 'What is the way out?'
> I opened my Bible to Isaiah 55: 7 and asked him to read it. He did so: 'Let the wicked forsake his way and the unrighteous man his thoughts, let him return to the Lord and he will abundantly pardon.'
> I said to him, 'The first part of that verse tells you what you must do, the second part tells you what God does.' I said, 'Are you prepared to do the first part?'
> He said, 'Yes I am.'
> 'Then if you are, God will have mercy and he will abundantly pardon.'
> Then this man said a tremendous thing, revealing that he was not trifling, but thinking seriously. 'I don't believe it,' he said. 'Do you mean God will forgive me and receive me now after all the failure of life to this point. I don't believe it. It's altogether too cheap.'
>
> I realized I was face to face with a soul conscious of need and in agony. I asked him, 'Have you been to work today?'
> 'Yes I've been down the pit.'
> 'How did you get to the surface to get home?'
> 'I went to the bottom of the shaft, got into the cage and was pulled up.'
> 'How much did you pay to come up?'
> 'Nothing.'
>
> Then staring at me, he abruptly said, 'Oh that won't do. I didn't pay anything to come up, but it cost the company...' And then, 'Oh my God, is that it? You mean forgiveness is free for me but it was not cheap for God?'

What that miner grasped then is the message God calls us to hear and to receive now. God's pardon is abundant and free. Why? Because the cost of you and me being brought up from the desolate pit of sin and death has been borne by our saviour, the Lord Jesus Christ. The cost is his sacrificial death on the cross. 'He redeemed your life from the pit, he forgives all your iniquities,' says the Psalmist. Why? Because he bore our sins in his death on the cross. 'He was wounded for our transgressions,' says Isaiah. Christ died for sins once for all. The righteous man dying for us unrighteous men. He did so to bring us to God, says the Apostle Peter. Pardoned. Forgiven. A free pardon includes a clear, clean conscience before God. A miner needs not only to be brought up from the coalpit, he needs to be washed clean so he may enjoy ordinary life again. Is that not a picture, a kind of picture of us all? Our Lord Jesus Christ brings us up from the pit of death, out into the light and life of God and in so doing he gives us a clean sheet. He blots out our transgressions. He creates a clean heart within. He washes away all our stain. Hearken diligently to that, hear that your soul may live. Seek the Lord while he is near.

40

Love Never Fails

At our local Detention Centre for young offenders we used to show a Christian film called 'Walls'. The title always raised a laugh. But those lads soon saw themselves in that film. It showed how barriers between people, living in the same house, can be much more difficult to get through than stone walls. They had lived in such homes, where walls of rejection had split the family. The concrete prison around them had been built from the wall of human sin at home.

Home can be a place where people seem to live apart in the same room. Walls of overwork and preoccupation come between you almost unnoticed. Conversation is reduced to: 'Oh, what do you want now? Can't you see I'm busy!' Before long you never do anything together.

And then it's too late, says the hit record, The Living Years:

> I wasn't there that morning
>   When my father passed away
> I didn't get to tell him
>   All the things I had to say
> Stilted conversations—
>   I'm afraid that's all we got.
> It's too late when we die
>   To admit we don't see eye to eye.
> Every generation blames the one before
> And all of their frustrations
>   come beating on your door.

The Lord has better things than that. Are we keeping doors open to one another, or are we erecting walls that end in estrangement and worse? Walls need doors. That film I mentioned focused on the Lord Jesus Christ as the door to reconciliation and love. He can open the way through the walls that cause us to collide and hurt each other.

Let's think about that.

The wall is a picture of how sin separates us from God and each other.

The door is a picture of salvation from sin and all that that can mean concerning access to God and openness to each other.

The barriers between us can be traced to our lost access to the love of God. Love never fails in the model family of the Trinity. The eternal love between God the Father, the Son, and the Holy Spirit gives us the pattern of life-long family love. But the wall of sin cuts off the human family from the source of this love. And so, the farther communities and families get from God—the creator and sustainer of the family—the more breakdown there is.

We need a door back, back to God and back home to each other. I found many years ago the truth of the old chorus:

> There's a way back to God from the dark paths of sin.
> There's a door that is open, and you may go in.
> At Calvary's cross is where you begin,
> When you come as a sinner to Jesus.

When Jesus Christ 'died for our sins and rose again from the dead,' he opened the door home to God.

Jesus speaks of Himself as the Open Door to the Father— whoever enters through him will be saved.

Our failure to grasp that good news is a very thick wall between us and God. Let me show you what I mean. You may know the story about the evangelist who went knocking on doors to talk to people about Jesus:

'I'm not interested in religion,' said a man who came to the door.

'Who mentioned religion?' said the visitor.

'You did.'

'No I didn't.

'Well, I'm not interested in church,' said the guy.

'Who mentioned church?'

'You did, didn't you?'

'I didn't,' said the visitor. 'I tell you what. Go back inside, shut the door, I'll ring the bell and let's start again.'

So the door opens again. 'Do you mind if I talked to you for a while about Jesus?'

'Still not interested,' said the longsuffering householder.

'What! Not interested in Jesus, the Son of God. What do you know about Him?'

'Died on a cross, didn't he?'

'Thousands died on a cross. Can you give me the name of anyone else who died on a cross?'

'Hm,' said the guy—and they started to talk about why Jesus had died.

The point at which that conversation opened up was the man's invitation to start again with Jesus. Jesus is a barrier breaker. He is our door to God, and through him doors can open between each other when they seem closed shut. When your love seems to be failing under the stresses at home, the love of God can find a way.

Let's look at some of the barriers love finds a way through. In all such family collisions there are walls of harsh anger and resentment. Harsh anger is cruel. We 'blow up' and have it out with others. Resentment hides inside and is just as cruel. We 'clam up' and have it in for them, and bitterness 'keeps a record of wrongs'.

> We open up a quarrel
>   Between the present and the past,
> We only sacrifice the future,
>   It's the bitterness that lasts.

The Bible faces up to these quarrels. 'Don't embitter your children and don't be harsh with your wife,' it says to us men. It takes every member of the family aside and says, 'A fool gives vent to his anger, but a wise man, holding it back, quietens it.'

Notice—we are told to 'hold back' anger, not 'hold it in'. Holding in anger is hidden resentment—those icy walls of silence. A wise man talks through the problem that has aroused his anger.

How? Quietening anger involves a soft answer, says the Bible. 'A soft answer turns away wrath.' God is giving us specific directions: a soft answer, not, no answer, not 'holding in'. Clamming up can be more infuriating than blowing up. 'Why don't you say something?' That only builds misunderstanding on top of the wall of sinful anger.

What kind of answer is a soft answer? Do you just give in feebly? No, a soft answer is not a weak answer.

A soft answer fits the need and aims at finding a solution to the problem between you. The Bible calls the tongue a rudder. It can steer you into worse storms. Or, it can aim at quietly working things out together so you can start again. A harsh answer attacks the other angry person and leads to more doors slamming, whereas the soft answer is prepared to be told, to be seen as the other sees us, to say sorry and start again, turning to God for his love that never fails.

But, you may say, how can the Bible state that love never fails when the world is littered with broken relationships?

It depends on what the Bible means by love.

Supposing, in that family crisis, everything had proceeded on the basis that love is only feelings. If love is only feelings, then love had failed. The feelings that ruled there were the high walls of anger, bitterness, fear.

But where do we get the idea that love is feelings?

From every edition of *Neighbours*, or any other soap: the film makers say love is feelings. They constantly expose you to the idea that love just happens. Feelings hit you and bowl you over. On television you see one looking at the other, you see it in their eyes, you know what's going to come, and wow! the music starts, and that is what love is…and it ain't half wonderful. It is. In its right place.

But how does the idea that love is only that, help a family like yours, when things have gone wrong? If love just happens, what happens to love when feelings change? What happens when feelings develop for someone else at work or round the corner?

The modern way of love says that's a signal for change. Love is getting what you feel like having. It doesn't seem to matter that children get sawn in half and that they have fragile feelings in all this too.

We shall look at two ways God helps us here.

Firstly, we need to hear what he says love is. Love is more than feelings. It's defined in 1 Corinthians 13. It involves not me getting, but me giving, doing good, being kind, patient, always persevering, always protecting. It involves action and commitment.

When relationships go sour and you end up hating the one you once thought you loved, it is no use waiting for tender feelings to return to motivate you to repair it. The one you live with has become your enemy.

True love, says Jesus, walks the way of giving, forgiving, and helping your enemy—even that one there in the kitchen, who you've decided to be rid of forever. Then wonderful things happen. Time and again you find feelings return when you do that considerate act that says, 'Sorry'. 'Love is a feeling to be learned'—learning to give our selves, our time, our heart, our help—whatever it takes to show love at the difficult point you now find yourself at.

Secondly, we need to see what God's love does for us, because I can hear you saying, 'What's going to make me give and forgive like that? You're right! We're like enemies in our house.

Well, the real problem is we are God's enemies too, every one of us. Our relationship to him is dead. God isn't dead, but we can live as if he is, just as we can cut people off as if they don't exist.

But God didn't leave things like that. He wants to bring us back home. And so the family love between Father and Son acted sacrificially to rescue enemies. 'Even while we were his enemies, Christ died for us.' It's we, the enemy, who deserve the righteous anger of God. But God's own Son took it, instead of us, on the cross. That arch enemy of Jesus, Saul of Tarsus, is amazed by it: 'The Son of God loved me and gave himself for me.' God forgives his enemies.

When we are enemies, we attack each other from behind walls of self defence, instead of tackling the problem between us. But God did not attack us. He tackled the real problem—our sin—himself. God was in Christ reconciling us to himself, making a way back, opening the door home.

The love that never fails is God's love. The effect of that love upon me, and upon my relationships with you brings down the walls. For when I take it in that God so loved me, I begin to take it in that God, likewise, loves you. If he does not reject you, am I to reject you? You may be the son or daughter who has gone off in a fury, the wife with the husband you feel you'd rather live without. When God forgives me and sends his love into my life, he calls me to a quality of living that teaches me to give and forgive, right there at home, where it is so needed. No love is like the love of Jesus. We can start again in him.

We began with walls between people.

Let's conclude this chapter with ceilings that are too low for people. When a great soprano sang in the home of Sibelius, he said to her—'My ceiling is too low for you.' When we live as families without God, living as if this world is all there is, we have too low a ceiling for harmony at home. We have too low a view of love. Under the cramping ceiling of materialism, love is crippled, for love is of God. Without the loving wisdom of God the Father, parents give up on their children and the family spirit is breaking. The love of Jesus can change that. 'For as high as the heavens are above the earth [no cramping ceiling there], so great is his everlasting love for those who trust him…he does not treat us as our sins deserve. Like a father has compassion on his children, so the Lord pities those who love him.'

41

Do You Want to Get Well?

Jesus turned up at Jerusalem at the height of the holiday season. The place he chose to go was not the entertainment areas or culture centres, but a bizarre hospital—the Pool of Bethesda—a place where chronic invalids gathered. It has been a symbol of healing ever since. For example, St Bartholomew's Hospital displays William Hogarth's painting of the scene at the Pool. The actual site is known to us because excavations in NE Jerusalem have uncovered it.

One Sabbath morning Jesus was to be found there, mingling with the crowd of waiting invalids. When the waters of the pool were stirred they were supposed to have healing properties, and the first to get in got healed—or so it was said. Many eyed those waters hopefully.

But there was one man there who felt utterly hopeless— paralysed for thirty-eight years. Oh, he had people to talk to and some obviously fed him or he wouldn't have lasted that long. But no one it seems, was prepared to stick with him to help him into the water. It was always somebody else. Never him. So he had given up.

He could have been a very unattractive character. From what we learn later, it seems as if his life, before illness overtook him, had been a moral mess. And what about thirty-eight years of no one being prepared to give him a hand? Did he have no gumption? Was he so miserable and self pitying? Did he show his bitterness so badly that people would not listen to him? How different that other paralytic, whose four friends were prepared to tear a slab off a flat roof to get their invalid friend to Jesus (Mark 2: 3–5).

Is this man a picture of our worst kind of tendency to be our own worst enemy by being so negative?

Well, however impossible this man was, the fact to grasp is that Jesus went for him—the most unattractive, the most chronic, the most depressed, the biggest challenge of all. And he once again turns this 'one off' miracle into a sign of his power to deal with our deepest spiritual need.

Let's follow the scene. The paralytic would, no doubt, have watched that Stranger moving among his fellow invalids. He had no idea who he was. Then, this Stranger moves towards him, singles him out and asks him a straight, strange question: 'Do you want to get well?' And he isn't willing to give a straight answer. He could have said: 'Do I want to? Why do you think I've been here all these years... Tell me how. Now!' But out stumbles his evasive reply. It even sounded as if he was blaming others that he wasn't better. 'Sir,' he said, 'I have none to help me.'

For many, that is a terrible true predicament. Many of you feel you can say that. The human drama of people living alone, suffering alone is part of our world. But listen. What about that stranger? It is because Jesus remains a stranger to so many today that so many feel they have none to help.

That day in Jerusalem, Jesus singled out just such a person. Straight into the paralysis of this man's hopelessness comes his command: 'Get up, pick up your mat and walk.' What must those around him have thought? How insensitive! He can't do that. The man's beyond help. It's impossible.

Exactly. Everything about the man symbolized deadness. But the word of the Son of God brings wholeness and life. The heart of a lifeless man leapt for joy. Now he wants what Jesus commands. And he's on his feet.

That physical miracle points to a message about eternal life. The miracles of John are also signs—signposts—that point beyond themselves. You haven't arrived when you come to a signpost. You go on to where it points. This sign points beyond the physical healing to our need of eternal life. The same power which in this miracle delivered that body from sickness is the power that grants you and me eternal life. That's what Jesus means when he later explains he, the Son of God, 'has power to give eternal life to whoever he pleased' (John 5: 24). How can it happen to you?

No one is too far gone for Jesus to restore. Look—this is what he says to us: 'Whoever hears my word and believes God who sent me, has eternal life and will not be condemned; he has crossed over from death to life' (John 5: 24).

The three commands to the paralytic—'Get up,' 'Pick up your mat,' 'Walk'—are paralleled by these other words addressed to us.

First, on hearing the call, 'Get up,' that man responded to the word of Christ. 'He believed' and his new life began. Similarly, 'Whoever hears my word and believes God who sent me, has eternal life.'

Next, 'Pick up your mat.' That mat represented all his past. All the condemning guilt association of those years of bitterness and self pity. That was past and over. Rolled up like his mat. So too, when you believe God sent his Son to be our Saviour, the promise 'He will not be condemned' sets your conscience free. 'The burden of (your) heart rolls away.' Your past is rolled up like that mat.

Then, 'Walk,' said Jesus. The first step of that walk is a picture of a greater change—the greatest change a man can ever know in this world. The change is this: 'he has crossed over from death to life' (John 5: 24).

To be made whole is as radical a change as that. There's a dividing line between death and life that you can walk across today. Even the dramatic change of paralysis one moment, walking the next, hardly conveys the momentous contrast. Earlier in this gospel he put it this way: 'For God so loved the world that he gave his only Son, that whoever believes in him shall not perish, but have everlasting life' (John 3: 16). If walking differs from paralysis, how much more everlasting life differs from perishing. Christ brings about a change in our relationship to God, as different as death from life.

'Do you want to be made whole?' said Christ to a man in the depths of hopelessness. He had no idea drastic change was possible. Maybe you say, 'Ah. If you only knew me; I'll never change. ' The lad out of detention centre doesn't want to go back, but he can't resist the smash and grab.

The husband whose uncontrollable temper is tearing the family to shreds, the lonely housewife secretly drinking and weaving a web of lies are all paralysed people. Change seems beyond them. But there is hope. It's a paralysed person we're talking about. And did he make himself whole? Our Lord's explanation of the miracle shows it's his power against your moral paralysis. 'The Son of God has power to give life to whoever he will.' That is hope for the worst.

During the unemployment of the 1930s, a man in Aberafon was drinking one Sunday in the Working Mén's Club. As usual he was alone. Like our paralytic, he had no one to help. His behaviour sickened most men. He heard two men at the next table talk about a local church and its preacher—'Yes, I was there last Sunday night, and the preacher said no one was hopeless.' The listener was all ears, and decided to go and hear if there was hope for him. It took him three weeks to pluck up enough courage to go into a church service. On that first hearing of the gospel, he understood, believed, and passed from condemnation to life. The transformation was remarkable. His face shone that night with radiance, as it did three years later when he died in the presence of his minister.

There are those who don't see how the question, 'Do you want to be made whole?' applies to them—hearty, robust, tough-minded, easy-going types. God diagnoses the condition of us all. The heart of every man, says the scripture, is sick. That Pool of Bethesda is a picture of the whole world lying stricken before God. The only hope is in Christ's hospital and to dismiss the diagnosis is another way of evading his question.

Imagine someone lying in a hospital bed. The doctor does his rounds. 'Well,' he says, 'I'm glad to tell you, we've got to the root of your trouble.'

'Trouble? What trouble doctor? There's nothing wrong with me. Try the guy in the next bed. I'm fine.'

As Christ, who knows our hearts, walks the wards of this world, stops, singles you out, identifies your problem, do you say 'Pass'?

'Whoever hears my word and believes God who sent me…has crossed over from death to life.'

Do you want to be made whole?

42

'The Bread of Life'

The lad we read about in John 6 must have been excited. He's been allowed to go off, all by himself, on a day's outing. Not to hear some rock band on tour, but to hear a preacher—Jesus.

We can imagine his mother saying, 'Now don't go without any food—you'll be away hours.' And so she packed two sardines and five small bread rolls. Before long he was part of a great crush of people—five thousand at least—and they hadn't had the foresight to bring any food. Perhaps he overheard Philip, one of the disciples, say to Jesus, 'Eight months wages wouldn't buy enough bread to feed all these.' 'Well, I've brought mine' he might have said, offering his packed lunch to Andrew.

Now Andrew was the sort of disciple who brought everything, big or small to the attention of Jesus—'there's a lad here with five small barley loaves.' It wasn't long before the astonished chap watched his five buns turn into a kind of bakery chain. Jesus took what he had given him, gave thanks, broke the bread and then kept on supplying the needs of everyone. What a story he would have when he got back home. Would they ever believe him?

Well, I wonder if you do? People seek ingenious ways of explaining away miracles like this. It's part of a constant attempt to reduce Jesus to our size, a superstar of course, but a 'man, just a man, like any other man.' Why? We don't keep on trying to prove Shakespeare and Socrates were mere men. That's obvious enough. So why Jesus? Because he so obviously isn't merely a man. The constant effort to down him to our level shows that he still hasn't been brought down—and neither will he. The way he explains the meaning of this miracle emphasises who he is.

So, let's ask what the miracle is pointing to, because we don't want to make the same mistake as most of those who were present. To them it meant one thing: they had found someone who could provide cheap and ready food. No wonder there begins an urgent popular movement to make him king and so Jesus has to elude them. That's not what his kingdom is about: and when they catch up with him a day later, he has to tell them that if they are interested in nothing more than material benefits then they are empty; dead men lacking the life of God.

'The truth is,' he says, 'You are looking for me because you ate the bread and had all you wanted, not because you understood the miracle' (John 6: 29).

He explains the miracle has two main purposes. It shows first, what he has come to give us, and secondly, what we must do to receive it. Let's look at them in turn.

First, what he has come to give us. 'I am the bread of life... the living bread that comes down from heaven. If a man eats of this bread he will live for ever. This bread is my flesh which I will give for the life of the world' (John 6: 35, 50–51).

Bread is basic. Phrases like 'the bread winner' and 'below the breadline' show us that. So, as bread is basic for everyday life—so Jesus is the basic necessity for everlasting life. If what he came to do was to give us that life, it follows that, without him, we do not have it. Let's elaborate on that. What sort of life does a man without Christ possess?

You may have cultivated tastes, prefer Bach to bingo, lament a society based on self-interest, help to feed the hungry, support green issues, want to protect children from nuclear disaster and preserve the quality of present and future life. But still Jesus says—what thought have you given to eternity? Did the Son of God come from eternity so we might continue to live as if this everyday life was everything? No one showed more compassion than he did. He fed the five thousand. Christians in a hungry world must keep on learning from that. But this miracle is the one he uses to tell us this life is not all. This world is not a dead end, 'only triviality for a moment and then nothing'. That is darkness. It is a demonstration of what Jesus means in this chapter- 'unless a man feeds on me he has no life in him.' There is a God we have to meet, and the life Jesus came to give us is so we might be prepared to meet him. He came to give us a loving, living relationship to God which, without him, we do not possess.

Receiving His Life

The second big question of this chapter is 'How do we receive his life? That bread was distributed to five thousand people, but each individual had to eat it. Bread is meant to be eaten, and no one else can eat for you.

So, Jesus, the bread of life, in a marvellous, miraculous way is given for a dying world. In order that we do not perish he has to be personally received. Jesus explains how in three phrases in chapter 6:

'He who believes in me…' (35b, 47);
'He who comes to me…' (35, 37);
'He who feeds on me shall live because of me' (51, 57).

Though that crowd had travelled miles to hear him, yet they had not come to him, Jesus says. To do that they, and we, must commit ourselves to him and accept him as the one who came from heaven that we might have life. To believe, to come, to feed, point to the same thing—we must take him for ourselves. Bread is nothing to do with our life until we partake it.

So what of you? Those five thousand people were elated at receiving food that lasted only until the next meal. But when Jesus said they must receive him if they would have life that lasted for ever, do you know what so many did? They went away. Why? Because they found his teaching too hard to accept. It was what he said about his death that they found too hard to take. 'This bread,' he said, 'is my flesh, which I give for the life of the world' (v. 51). Jesus, the bread of life, is himself broken before we share in him. Have you taken in this meaning? To share his life we must come to him as the saviour who died for us. From the same people who had broken and eaten those barley loaves he now demanded a spiritual response. 'Unless a man feed on me, he has no life in him.' Many proved they couldn't take it. They turned away from him.

Now people have always found these sort of statements hard to take. They seem too crude for some refined tastes. But was the death of Christ refined? We have two kinds of bread in our day. One is over refined, with the rough and hard bits taken out. We have discovered it lacks nutrition, indeed it doesn't do us all that much good. We have learned our lesson and the old, wholewheat bread is in again, the rough and the hard included.

There's an old story of a rugged cross with hard nails, driven by rough men into those same caring carpenter hands that had fed hungry crowds. We find it hard to see that there, at Calvary, the Son of God gave himself for us. But the bread of life does not come to us refined of the hard things that give us life. He comes to us as bread from heaven. 'He came down to earth from heaven who is God and Lord of all,' says the carol. Yes! God. You can't refine that away from the bread of life. We receive him as the saviour who gave his life for sinners—hard as that is for us to swallow.

But not everyone turned away. Far from it. So what about you? When our Lord asked the disciples 'Will you also go away?' Peter shows he has fed deeply on our Lord's words. 'Lord' he said, 'to whom else can we go? You have the words of eternal life.' You can go to many others for many other things, but if you hunger for eternal life, there is but one source of supply.

In some areas of the world, where food is scarce, people greet each other not with 'How are you?' but 'Have you eaten yet?' I greet you in Jesus' name and ask, 'Have you eaten yet of the food that sustains to eternal life? That bread is not scarce, but you must seek it at its source. That means coming with the empty hand of faith and taking life from Jesus.

Have you spiritual taste for this bread? If not, God grant you may see what you are missing. Today, for you, in the midst of life perhaps so preoccupied with other things that you have been oblivious to your hunger, may there come a taste for the gift of God.

> O taste and see that God is good
> Blessed is the man who trusts in him.

Life's End or New Beginnings?

43

Saturday Night and Sunday Morning

The way we spend Saturday night and Sunday morning says a lot about our lives. A stroll through city streets on a carefree Saturday night would leave us uneasy. Night fun time leaves many broken people in awful loneliness.

And what then of Sunday morning? A boring non-event? A shaking off the hangover? Letting it out on the golf ball?

God has so much better for both days. Saturday and Sunday can be delightful twins, speaking of the harmony and integration of our lives in time and for eternity.

Saturday is the last day of the week, which reminds us that one day this marvellous but decaying world God created will itself have its last day. On Saturday we celebrate and refresh our mortal humanity. Its span is brief, so we make time for friends, family, leisure, play.

But Saturday, the old Sabbath day of rest, is lived in the light of Sunday, the first day, the new day of Christ's resurrection, the day that points to a new heaven and a new earth, where there will be no time limits. On Sunday we renew and review our eternal inheritance, with all that means for our daily wholeness. We rejoice in the Saviour on the Lord's Day, giving thanks for our new life in him, a day for mending relationships with him and each other, so easily soiled by sin. Promises and commitments are strengthened in God. It's a day to put on clean clothes of love and forgiveness in Christ, reminding ourselves that

we need them every day. Saturday and Sunday represent
the blessings God gives to us with his left hand and his
right hand—gifts of fun and fellowship, play and prayer.
God is Lord of both days, and every day. For everything
God created is good, to be received with thanksgiving by
all who believe and know the truth. The joys of physical
recreation and spiritual re-creation go together where
Christ is worshipped from the heart.

Without that dimension, what would it be, asks the poet
John Donne, if this Saturday night were not just the last
night of the week, but the world's last night?

> The day of the Lord will come like a thief in the night…
> But you, brothers, are not in darkness so that this day
> should surprise you like a thief. You are all sons of the
> light and sons of the day. We do not belong to the night
> or to the darkness. So then, let us not be like others, but
> let us be alert and self controlled. Those who get drunk
> get drunk at night. But since we belong to the day, let's be
> self-controlled, putting on faith and love as a breastplate,
> and the hope of salvation as a helmet. For God did
> not appoint us to suffer wrath but to receive salvation
> through our Lord Jesus Christ who died for us so we
> may live with him.

Celebrating Sunday as the Lord's Day means facing the
Bible's message of the Last Day. Both perspectives are what
we need to integrate our confused, fragmented, yet driven
lives. For the past six days we have lived in a world that
rushes and relaxes, eats, sleeps, laughs, cries, loves, and
squabbles. Burials, birthdays, obscenities, heroism—what
is it all about? If we tumble again into tomorrow in the same
way we have spun through the other six, we start the week
with that Monday morning feeling of 'here we go again'…
and we've never stopped to think what life is all about.

So, Sunday worship is a glad and voluntary interruption.
It breaks our treadmill routine. It helps us recognize that,
at any moment, there may be a mandatory interruption of
our lives: God's light shining upon the hiddenness of our
motives and actions, Saturday nights included. To worship
the Lord in the beauty of holiness on Sunday gets us into
a training programme of practical holiness for every other
day until the Last.

44

A Judge Named Jesus

Imagine you lived some two thousand years ago in Galilee. Time and again you've been gripped by the sayings of a young Jewish teacher called Jesus. He's a compelling story teller, and you've found his penetrating wisdom driving home lessons to your heart with the force of eternal truths, challenging, comforting. But there's also something profoundly discomforting about him that bugs you. Now and again he says that one day he, the Son of Man as he called himself, will judge the nations of the world, and he will judge them on how they have treated him and his followers.

> When the Son of Man comes in his glory…all the nations will be gathered before him, and he will separate the people one from another as a shepherd separates the sheep from the goats. He will put the sheep on his right and the goats on his left.
>
> Then the King will say to those on his right, 'Come, you who are blessed by my Father, take your inheritance, the kingdom prepared for you since the creation of the world. For I was hungry and you gave me something to eat, I was thirsty and you gave me something to drink, I was a stranger and you invited me in, I needed clothes and you clothed me, I was sick and you looked after me, I was in prison and you came to visit me.'
>
> Then the righteous will answer him, 'Lord, when did we see you hungry and feed you, or thirsty and give you

something to drink? When did we see you a stranger and invite you in, or needing clothes and clothe you? When did we see you sick or in prison and go to visit you?'

The King will reply, 'I tell you the truth, whatever you did for one of the least of these brothers of mine, you did for me.'

Matt. 25: 31ff

Two thousand years after Jesus told this famous story about himself and the nations, here we are retelling it in days of its partial fulfilment. This storyteller has stirred the nations deeply—by now people out of every nation have come to him, moved to practical discipleship by this beautiful story of spontaneous, unaffected care for the destitute. There is challenge and comfort in it.

But there is discomfort in it too. The story itself still points ahead for fulfilment—someone will be there to meet us all at the world's last day. A Judge named Jesus.

As always, the crisis we have in listening to Jesus is that matters come back to the old question: What good man could keep on telling you that your eternity depended on your relationship to him? Either he is both God and man, or he is not a good man at all. No other religious or moral leader speaks about himself as he does.

This story is just one of countless New Testament examples that bring together these unique claims and credentials of Jesus as God who became man. As Judge of the nations, he makes final declarations about our eternal destiny—'to the right'; 'to the left'. Yet this divine judge is entirely devoid of harshness. He acts with the infinite sympathy of the Son of Man who suffered here among us and feels the afflictions of his brothers as though they were his own: 'whatever you did for these brethren of mine, you did for me.'

That criterion of judgement is startling: How have we treated Jesus in the vulnerable persons who are his followers? The nations are judged on their response to the followers of Jesus, because that is what indicates their response to Jesus the Judge himself.

What a searchlight that will put on the history of nations.

45

The Dark Invader

The arena of conflict featuring Luke Sky Walker, Darth Vador, the Force, and the Empire is one of many sagas that try to convey the tussle in the universe between good and evil, light and darkness, God and Satan. It's as if the memory of the race, in a distorted but persistent way, throws up some recollection of the true cause of conflict between law and lawlessness. The Bible book of Revelation gives a picture of the real causes behind our human predicament:

> And there was war in heaven...the great dragon was hurled down—that ancient serpent called the devil or Satan, who leads the whole world astray. He was hurled to the earth, and his angels with him. Then I heard a loud voice in heaven say: 'Now have come the salvation and the power and the kingdom of God and the authority of Christ. For the accuser of our brothers, who accuses them before God day and night has been hurled down. They overcame him by the blood of the Lamb and by the word of their testimony; they did not love their lives so much as to shrink from death. Therefore rejoice, you heavens and you who dwell in them! But woe to the earth and sea because the devil has gone down to you! He is filled with fury because he knows his time is short.'
>
> Rev. 12: 7a, 9–12

This tells how it came about that an opposing force arose to battle it out with the rightful ruler of the universe, the emperor beyond the sea of time and space.

'And there was war in heaven...'

The hostile force is overcome by the Ruler, but, as a defeated, alien empire, it strikes back. A dark invader penetrates the unique outpost of the rightful Lord—Planet Earth—an inhabited space island in this cosmic sea of time and space.

The colony of God—his image bearers, created in his likeness—is overcome, deceived by the lie, and the outpost is overrun. The world is led astray. The alien force spreads destruction and confusion wherever it infiltrates.

But all is not lost. The God of the universe retains communication. From the control centre come sporadic promises to liberate. There are those who believe it and reject the lie, sometimes at great personal cost.

Then, after millennia of raised expectations and dashed hopes, the captive territory is visited, incognito, by the Son of the Lord. He comes to take on the dark invader. Through apparent defeat and death, and then a sensational comeback to life, he gains the decisive initiative in the conflict. The new age dawns. He offers liberty to all who will follow him in anticipation that the dark invader will finally be overthrown.

A freedom fighter movement gains ground behind the lines. Its aim is not sabotage. Its weapons are truth and love. Its a battle for the minds and hearts of people in a bent world, so bent that the idea of the true Lord is dismissed. Sometimes his ever-growing band of followers give the Invader mocking ammunition. They too, fail and fall out. And it adds to the dark persuasive propaganda.

But while they put their faith in truth from headquarters and act consistently on the written words of communication, the cause advances. Their two-way communication is their constant means of supply in the continuing conflict. They work for and wait for deliverance. The end is never in doubt even in their darkest hour.

He is coming back. Rejoice. Hold on—to the end and the new beginning.

46

The Lord is King

The Lord is King, lift up thy voice,
O earth, and all ye heavens rejoice!
From world to world the joy shall ring,
'The Lord omnipotent is King.'

Josiah Conder, the author of this hymn, was born in 1789, the year of the French Revolution. He grew up in a world of colossal instability. The old order crumbled. Rulers toppled all over Europe. Later in life, when he was a newspaper editor, Conder was more concerned about how revolution had tried to dethrone God. Men's pens were busy announcing his death and giving glory to man in the highest. We have grown used to it.

Conder was unimpressed. He knew man's unbelief is sure to err. To resist God, distrust Him, 'to murmur at his wise decrees and doubt his royal promises' was to take issue with 'the Judge of all the earth' who is not only just and true, but omnipotent.

The hymn sings of security in life and death. Even if the old order of this world crumbles, though hills tremble and high mountains melt away, even then 'Your God is King, your Father reigns' and the 'Man of love, the crucified' reigns with him. He has secured life and a new world for you.

'He reigns! Ye saints, exalt your strains'
Your God is King, your Father reigns
And he is at the Father's side,
the Man of love, the Crucified.

Original Broadcasts

The chapters in this book were broadcast originally as the following programmes:

1. BBC Radio Wales, Word for the Week. A week when all UK nationwide religious broadcasts came from Wales.
2. BBC Radio Wales, Weekend Word.
3. BBC Radio 4, Five Talks, Prayer for the Day.
4. BBC Radio 4, Five Talks, Prayer for the Day.
5. BBC World Service, Reflections.
6. BBC World Service, Reflections.

7-12. BBC Radio Wales, Six Talks, Weekend Word.

13. BBC Radio Wales, Celebration, broadcast from Whitefield Presbyterian Church, Abergavenny.
14. BBC Radio Wales, Celebration, broadcast from the Chapel of the University of Wales School of Medicine, Cardiff. It was led by members of the medical Staff and the congregation from Highfields Free Church, Cardiff, was joined by members of the Cambrensis Choir.
15. BBC Radio Wales, Celebration, from the same venue.
16. (a) BBC Radio Wales, Christmas Morning Celebration broadcast from St Asaph's Cathedral in Clwyd, N Wales. The choir sang nine carols.
    (b) BBC Radio Wales, Weekend Word.
    (c) BBC Radio 4, The Daily Service.
17. BBC Radio 2, Five Talks, Pause for Thought.
18. (a) BBC Radio Wales, Celebration Easter Series.
    (b) BBC Radio Wales, Celebration Easter Series.
    (c) BBC Radio Wales, Celebration Easter Series. Broadcast from Whitefield Presbyterian Church, Abergavenny on three consecutive Sundays.
19. (a) BBC Radio 4, Prayer for the Day, Ascension Week.
    (b) BBC Radio 4, Prayer for the Day, Ascension Week.

(c) BBC Radio 4, Prayer for the Day, Ascension Week.

(d) BBC Radio 4, Prayer for the Day, Ascension Day.

20. BBC Radio Wales, Live Phone-in Programme to consider the role and mission of the Christian church.

21. BBC Radio Wales, Weekend Word.

22-3. BBC Radio Wales, Weekend Word.

24. BBC Radio 4, Four Talks, Prayer for the Day.

25. BBC Radio 2, Pause for Thought.

26. BBC World Service, Reflections.

27-9. BBC Radio Wales, Weekend Word.

30. BBC Radio Wales , Weekend Word.

31. BBC Radio 2, Pause for Thought.

32. BBC World Service, Reflections.

33. BBC World Service, Reflections.

34. BBC Radio Wales, Weekend Word.

35. BBC Radio 2. Pause for Thought. Four talks. I am indebted to Ian Barclay's study of Psalm 23, 'He is everything to me', Falcon, 1972

36. BBC Radio 4, Four Talks, Prayer for the Day

37. (a) BBC Radio Wales, Celebration. A programme on evangelical hymn writers of the 18th century. Isaac Watts, Charles Wesley, John Newton, William Williams, with a hymn of each.

    (b) BBC Radio 2, Pause for Thought. This study of the hymns of Williams Pantycelyn, marking his bicentenary, was given in a series of four programmes. Each concluded with one of his hymns.

38. BBC Radio 4, Sunday Morning Service broadcast live from Whitefield Presbyterian Church, Abergavenny.

39. BBC Radio 4, Sunday Morning Service broadcast live from Whitefield Presbyterian Church, Abergavenny.

40. BBC Radio 4, Sunday Morning Service broadcast live from Highfields Free Church, Cardiff.

41. BBC 1 Television Sunday Morning Worship.

42. BBC 1 Television Sunday Morning Worship. These two sermons on John 5 and John 6 were part of services provided by Glenwood Community Church, Llanedeyrn, Cardiff, for TV's nationwide Sunday Morning Worship. They were part of a series entitled, 'The Word - A Journey through John's Gospel.'

43. BBC Radio 4, Ten to Ten, Saturday Night.

44. BBC Radio 4, Prayer for the Day.

45. BBC Radio 4, Prayer for the Day.

46. BBC Radio 2, the final hymn of Sunday Half Hour broadcast from Moriah Baptist Church, Risca.